T0334110

'Well known for his work on Fromm, Laing, Erikson and Karl Stern, Daniel Burston's book makes an important contribution to the lingering controversies concerning Jung's anti-Semitism and similar stereotypes in the post-Jungian movement. It raises important questions, such as why there is no convincing Jungian explanation for anti-Semitism as a collective phenomenon, nor how to treat it within analysis. Anyone interested in Jung or the history of analytical psychology should read this fine work.'

Henry Abramovitch, *Founding President, Israel Institute of Jungian Psychology; Professor Emeritus, Tel Aviv University, Israel*

'*Anti-Semitism and Analytical Psychology* is an in-depth study of different kinds of anti-Semitism, and the history of Jung's and the Zürich Jungians' ambivalent attitudes towards Judaism and Zionism. Highly recommended for everyone interested in sifting the gold of truthfulness from falsehood, and fact from fiction.'

Ann Casement, LP, FRAI, FRSM, *Professor, Oriental Academy of Analytical Psychology, China*

'In this new controversial book, Daniel Burston does with Jung what Heidegger's followers feared most – an analysis of the Jewish question in the shadow of Nazism. For Jungian apologists, this is a controversial critique and unwelcome trespass; for others, a sober corrective. Here Burston stands out as the premier authority on interrogating the specter of anti-Semitism lurking in the closet of Analytical Psychology.'

Jon Mills, *Emeritus Professor of Psychology and Psychoanalysis; Faculty, Postgraduate Programs in Psychoanalysis & Psychotherapy, Adelphi University, U.S.A.; author,* Debating Relational Psychoanalysis

'Burston sets the still-troubling question of Jung's anti-Semitism within the frame of a robust and succinct historical, cultural and political analysis of Jew-hatred in general. Thinking about the existing literature, I believe this is a unique achievement. Today's post-Jungians, many of whom retreat behind the mantra "a man of his times", really need to read this account which is balanced, sincere and oriented to the phenomenon of anti-Semitism in the future as well as in the past and present. Those who stand outside the Jungian community might also find the book illuminating.'

Professor Andrew Samuels, *Series Editor and author,* The Political Psyche

Anti-Semitism and Analytical Psychology

Carl Jung angrily rejected the charge that he was an anti-Semite, yet controversies concerning his attitudes toward Jews, Zionism and the Nazi movement continue to this day. This book explores Jung's ambivalent relationship to Judaism in light of his career-changing relationship and rupture with Sigmund Freud and takes an unflinching look at Jung's publications, public pronouncements and private correspondence with Freud, James Kirsch and Erich Neumann from 1908 to 1960.

Analyzing the religious and racial, Christian and Muslim, high-brow and low-brow varieties of anti-Semitism that were characteristic of Jung's time and place, this book examines how Muslim anti-Semitism and anti-Zionism intensified following the Balfour Declaration (1917), fostering the resurgence of anti-Semitism on the Left since the fall of the Soviet Empire. It urges readers to be mindful of the new and growing threats to the safety and security of Jewish people posed by the resurgence of anti-Semitism around the world today.

This book explores the history of the controversy concerning Jung's anti-Semitism both before and after the publication of *Lingering Shadows: Jungians, Freudians and Anti-Semitism* (1991), and invites readers to reflect on the relationships between Judaism, Christianity and Zionism, and between psychoanalysis and analytical psychology, in new and challenging ways. It will be of considerable interest to psychoanalysts, historians and all those interested in the history of analytical psychology, anti-Semitism and interfaith dialogue.

Daniel Burston, Ph.D., is the author of numerous books and journal articles on the history of psychoanalysis, psychiatry and psychology, with a special focus on where and how these fields converge, overlap and intertwine with politics, religion and philosophy (and with one another) historically.

Routledge Focus on Jung, Politics and Culture

The Jung, Politics and Culture series showcases the 'political turn' in Jungian and Post-Jungian psychology. Established and emerging authors offer unique perspectives and new insights as they explore the connections between Jungian psychology and key topics – including national and international politics, gender, race and human rights.

For a full list of titles in this series, please visit www.routledge.com/Focus-on-Jung-Politics-and-Culture/book-series/FJPC

Titles in the series:

From Vision to Folly in the American Soul: Jung, Politics and Culture
Thomas Singer

Vision, Reality and Complex: Jung, Politics and Culture
Thomas Singer

Anti-Semitism and Analytical Psychology: Jung, Politics and Culture
Daniel Burston

Anti-Semitism and Analytical Psychology
Jung, Politics and Culture

Daniel Burston

Routledge
Taylor & Francis Group

LONDON AND NEW YORK

First published 2021
by Routledge
2 Park Square, Milton Park, Abingdon, Oxon OX14 4RN

and by Routledge
605 Third Avenue, New York, NY 10158

Routledge is an imprint of the Taylor & Francis Group, an informa business

© 2021 Daniel Burston

The right of Daniel Burston to be identified as author of this work has been
asserted by him in accordance with sections 77 and 78 of the Copyright,
Designs and Patents Act 1988.

All rights reserved. No part of this book may be reprinted or reproduced or utilised
in any form or by any electronic, mechanical, or other means, now known or
hereafter invented, including photocopying and recording, or in any information
storage or retrieval system, without permission in writing from the publishers.

Trademark notice: Product or corporate names may be trademarks or registered
trademarks, and are used only for identification and explanation without
intent to infringe.

British Library Cataloguing-in-Publication Data
A catalogue record for this book is available from the British Library

Library of Congress Cataloging-in-Publication Data
A catalog record has been requested for this book

ISBN: 978-0-367-42673-6 (hbk)
ISBN: 978-0-367-42674-3 (pbk)
ISBN: 978-0-367-85431-7 (ebk)

DOI: 10.4324/9780367854317

Typeset in Times New Roman
by Newgen Publishing UK

For my father, Baruch ("Benny") Burston
"Bis a hunderdt und tzvanzig!"

Contents

Acknowledgments

I wish to convey my sincere thanks and appreciation to Ann Casement, Nathan Greenfield Jon Mills and Henry Abramovitch for reading and responding so knowledgably to my manuscript in progress, and to Andrew Samuels for soliciting it in the first place. Thanks also to my editor at Routledge, Susannah Frearson. Finally, thanks all my colleagues in Duquesne University's Jewish Studies Forum, and my friends and supporters in the International Association of Jungian Studies.

Introduction

Next to Sigmund Freud, Carl Gustav Jung was the single most important and influential figure in the history of psychoanalysis. Yet Jung seldom gets the credit he deserves among the Freudian faithful, because after their falling out, Freud's followers were afraid of acknowledging even the slightest intellectual kinship with Freud's disciple-turned-adversary (Burston, 2003). To do so was considered an act of betrayal or of intellectual weakness. Consequently, when they were influenced by Jung, Freud's followers were careful to conceal that fact from others, and often, indeed, from themselves (Roazen, 2002).

One reason for their reticence on this score is that Jung was widely reputed to be an anti-Semite and was charged by Freud's followers with having collaborated with the Nazis (Burston, 2003). Indeed, in *The Jungians: A Comparative and Historical Perspective*, Thomas Kirsch points out:

> In today's world of psychotherapy, one cannot be a Jungian without having to answer the charge that Jung was both a Nazi and anti-Semitic ... His statements on the over-materialistic values of Jewish psychology, and its corrosive effects on the spiritual nature of the psyche, were made in the 1930s; the timing of these statements could not have been worse. The debate that has raged over what Jung meant by these statements goes on unabated. Every time that the issue is raised anew, clarification and amplification of Jung's statements are made, but the issue refuses to die ... Psychoanalysts have used it as a reason not to study Jung; other intellectuals use it as a reason to discredit Jung. Every candidate and analyst, Jew or non-Jew, has to come to terms with this aspect of Jung for him/her self, and at present roughly one third of Jungian analysts in the world do have a Jewish background.
>
> (Kirsch, 2000, p. 132)

Later in this book, Kirsch explains that several German-Jewish men were forced to flee Germany in the early 1930s, and subsequently settled in London, Rome, New York, Los Angeles and Tel Aviv, where they started Analytical Psychology Clubs and, in due course, training Institutes.[1] One of them was Kirsch's father, James Kirsch, who vigorously defended Jung against the charge of anti-Semitism. Nevertheless, even Thomas Kirsch concedes that

> Earlier generations of Jungians simply defended Jung unequivocally... (and) the continuing controversy around this remains an obstacle to Jung's greater acceptance world-wide.
>
> (Kirsch, 2000, p. 243)

So, Jews were instrumental in disseminating Jung's ideas internationally before WWII, and roughly one-third of Jungian analysts today are of Jewish heritage. That being so, could the charges of anti-Semitism really be true? Marga Speicher, a Jungian training analyst in San Antonio, Texas, certainly thinks so. In "Jung, Anti-Semitism and the Nazi Regime" she urged Jungians:

> to give the necessary recognition and acknowledgement to Jung's shadow, his anti-Semitism, his fascination with archetypal energies, and his apolitical stance as well as the shadow of the Jungian community in those very same matters. We have to ask ourselves continually 1) Where do the underground waters of ethnocentrism, anti-Semitism and racism flow at the present time? 2) When and where does our recognition of archetypal energies turn into fascination and cause us to lose sight of earthly reality? 3) Where do we claim an apolitical stance in a rather routine manner without due consideration of the political impact of such a position?
>
> Such an exploration ... can lead us ... to a better understanding of shadow, personal and archetypal, individual and collective, and ... of the ever present pitfalls inherent in personal and communal life as well as ... the theoretical and philosophical positions we hold.
>
> (Speicher, 1991, pp. 338–339)

So, Speicher's program for the Jungian community is to use the study of Jung's anti-Semitism as a prelude to a kind of deeper collective self-study; one that insures that the mistakes of the past are not repeated when racism and ethnocentrism rear their ugly heads, as they have done so alarmingly in the past few years. The goals of this study are aligned with hers, though I am not Jungian analyst, and do not frame my findings primarily in Jungian terms. Nor do I apologize on this score. I am an historian of the behavioral sciences, and console myself that others can translate my ideas into Jungian terminology more capably than I, and that before this happens, many Jungians *need* to step outside the Jungian frame of reference temporarily to see the whole issue in its true dimensions anyway.

None of the texts or findings presented here are new. However, they are synthesized and presented in new ways that challenge readers to reflect on the scope and severity of the issues we're addressing. After reading this book, perhaps Jungians will grasp why so many Jews think of anti-Semitism as a shape-shifting but deathless adversary that lives forever in the hidden recesses of Christian and Muslim cultures; one that lies dormant for shorter or longer periods, but always returns to torment us through the ages. Are we too sensitive or too defensive at times? Yes, no doubt, some are. But the charge that we are too quick to worry or take offense is often hurled precisely when we are teetering on the brink of another shattering catastrophe, as was the case with Jung and his circle in the early 1930s.

That said, there is now considerable disagreement was to what anti-Semitism actually is. Indeed, conversations about the origins, nature and scope of anti-Semitism can be very contentious nowadays. Why so? Well, for one thing, the experts themselves often offer divergent definitions of (and explanations for) anti-Semitism. Moreover, many people angrily repudiate the suggestion that they are anti-Semitic, though their attitudes and behavior strongly suggest otherwise. That being so, for the sake of simplicity, we will define anti-Semitism simply as an irrational belief that by virtue of their faith and/or heredity, Jews pose an actual or potential threat to the safety, security and/or ethical integrity on their non-Jewish neighbors, presumably by seeking (or sustaining) an unfair advantage or attempting to damage or devalue their non-Jewish neighbors behind the scenes, often through (alleged) conspiracies of various kinds. In such cases, the magnitude of the perceived threat varies with the intensity of anti-Semitic sentiments, rather than according to any actual or intrinsic qualities of the people who are feared and despised. Anti-Semitic beliefs and attitudes are then used to justify anti-Semitic practices, ranging from casual disdain (low intensity) to fierce discrimination (high intensity), and from there to occasional episodes of violence that may escalate into genocidal campaigns.

After reading this book, perhaps readers will think differently about anti-Semitism than they did beforehand, and will seek to clarify – for themselves and with others – how to interpret and address different varieties of anti-Semitism in their own communities more effectively. What role can Analytical Psychology play in understanding, addressing and alleviating the complex and worrisome social realities described in the following pages? Very little, unless Jungians grasp the sprawling complexities of anti-Semitism in historical perspective, as an outgrowth of centuries-long interfaith and intercultural conflicts that persist to this day. Furthermore, Jungians must grapple candidly with the history of anti-Semitism *within* Analytical Psychology, and not just society at large. The purpose of this book is to provide an introduction to both of these topics, furnishing students and practitioners of Analytical Psychology with a new way of seeing things; one that will enliven and inform debates on these issues going forward.

Note

1 The first Jungian training institute was cofounded by Joseph Wheelwright and Joseph Henderson in San Francisco in 1943. The London institute opened in 1945, and the Zürich institute opened in 1948.

References

Burston, D. 2003. "Sanity, Madness and the Sacred in C.G. Jung and R.D.Laing". *Harvest: International Journal for Jungian Studies*, 2003, vol. 49, #2, pp. 70–92.

Kirsch, T. 2000. *The Jungians: A Comparative and Historical Perspective.* London: Routledge.

Roazen, P. 2002. *The Trauma of Freud: Controversies in Psychoanalysis.* New Brunswick, NJ: Transaction Press.

Speicher, M. 1991. "Jung, Anti-Semitism and the Nazi Regime." In Maidenbaum, A. and Martin, S. *Lingering Shadows: Freudians, Jungians and Anti-Semitism.* New York: Shamabala.

1 Anti-Semitism in historical context

Varieties of anti-Semitism

No matter how you define it, anti-Semitism is an old and remarkably persistent form of ethnic and religious prejudice. Scholars have found evidence of anti-Semitic attitudes in pre-Christian Hellenistic and Roman authors (e.g. Manetho, Tacitus, Ovid) and among pagan-Gnostic authors of the second- and third-century CE (e.g. Mani, Basilides). Anti-Semitic ideas and utterances are also found in the New Testament and the writings of the Church Fathers, including Bishop Melito of Sardis, Marcion, St. Ambrose, St. Augustine and St. John Chrysostom, among others. By the late Middle Ages, by and large, Christian anti-Semites believed that Jews are a distinct "race", often with specific "racial characteristics", such as darker skin and hair, a large, hooked nose and a grasping, materialistic disposition, and a decidedly tribal outlook that is the opposite of the noble Christian ideal, which aspires to spiritual universality. Indeed, they rejected Jesus as the Messiah and were (allegedly) responsible for his crucifixion because they possess these odious (physical and spiritual) characteristics (Burston, 2014).

Nevertheless, Christians generally believed that despite the stigma associated with their ancestry, Jews could be "saved" if they converted to Christianity. To deny Jews this chance at redemption would place limits on God's powers of forgiveness, and therefore amount to heresy. By contrast with his religious counterpart, the newer, racist anti-Semite claimed that we are beyond redemption, because our questionable characteristics were never simply a matter of belief, but are indelibly inscribed in our genes. According to the Nazis, for example, one's actual faith (or the lack of it) is utterly irrelevant. You could be a devout Catholic, like the Carmelite nun, St. Edith Stein. But if you had one Jewish grandparent, you were labeled Jewish and transported to a death camp in due course.

Nevertheless, despite some striking differences – the older, religious variety of anti-Semitism favoring conversion, the newer, essentialist form opposing it vehemently on grounds of "racial hygiene" – there were some similarities between religious and racial anti-Semitism. First, there is a thread of continuity that links religious to racial anti-Semitism; an obsession with "pure blood" that arose after Spanish Inquisition, and the collective paranoia surrounding Marranos or *conversos*; the many thousands of Jews who were forcibly converted to Christianity and were widely suspected of plotting to subvert the (supposedly) ideal Christian kingdom (Williamson, 1989; Carroll, 2001).

Another common feature of religious and racial anti-Semitism is that they both malign and dehumanize Jews, yet hold them responsible for their own suffering, essentially blaming the victim. Moreover, both spawn bizarre collective fantasies about Jewish conspiracies. In medieval times, Jews were alleged to kill Christian children for their blood at Passover, and held responsible for bringing famine and Bubonic plague. These vicious rumors followed Jews everywhere, and as feudalism crumbled, started to take on new forms. In 1903, for example, the Czarist police concocted a phony document called *The Protocols of the Elders of Zion* which purportedly "proved" the existence of a worldwide Jewish conspiracy to dominate the world by taking over banks and the media (Cohn, 1996.) This book sold millions of copies around the world, and continues to inspire fear and hatred of Jews to this very day.

In a series of influential books and articles, historian Gavin Langmuir argued that collective phantasies concerning the Jews in the Middle Ages constituted a qualitative shift away from the *adversos Judaeos* tradition of earlier Christianity, because they are so radically estranged from reality and are unparalleled elsewhere in the history of the West. By contrast, he claims, the anti-Jewish prejudices of the Church Fathers generated cognitive distortions and exaggerations no different and no worse than garden variety forms of ethnic and religious prejudice, given the temper of times. The virulent anti-Semitism we encounter today, he claims, really began with the (alleged) crucifixion of young William of Norwich by Jews in 1144; a hateful rumor that unleashed a torrent of false accusations, culminating in the blood libel against the Jews for the death of "Little Saint Hugh" of Lincoln in 1255, resulting in the total expulsion of Jews from England by edict of King Edward in 1290 (Langmuir, 1990; Smith, 1996).

Langmuir's claim has been challenged by scholars who argue that the roots of Western anti-Semitism can already be found in the New Testament, where Jews are often characterized as a deicidal, deceitful people, or as children and agents of the devil (Crossan, 1996; Ruether,

1997; Carroll, 2001). Though open to doubt, however, Langmuir's thesis merits close attention, because the distinction he made between garden variety prejudice, which engenders relatively minor cognitive distortions, and the bizarre collective fantasies that populate the modern anti-Semitic imaginary has occurred to other researchers. As Langmuir (and others) point out, many contemporary anti-Semites are not merely prejudiced. They are utterly impervious to evidence or rational argument, enabling those who share their frame of reference to entertain wildly antithetical ideas and beliefs without the slightest regard for facts or for logical consistency. As Stephen Bronner points out:

> The imagined Jewish conspiracy permeates every aspect of the totality, and it is identified with both sides of every contradiction. Capitalists and socialists are not "really" opposed, for example, but rather manipulated by the same puppet master.
> … The Jew can symbolize fabulous wealth and degraded poverty, rebellion and miserliness and excess, capitalism and communism, the provincialism of the ghetto and the power of a world-wide conspiracy, and – above all – the "hidden hand" of a conspiracy threatening the good-hearted though hapless Christian *man of the people*.
>
> (Bronner, 2020)

So to underscore the importance of *chimeria* as a potent factor in contemporary anti-Semitism, and to differentiate them from milder (if not necessarily older) forms of prejudice, it may be useful to differentiate (in a purely descriptive fashion) between low-brow/high-intensity anti-Semites and high-brow/low-intensity anti-Semites. The former are often semi-literate, manifestly incoherent or irrational, and deal in bizarre conspiracy theories and lurid stereotypes, attempting to incite the masses directly (e.g. Adolf Hitler). By contrast, the latter type tend to avoid – and often profess to deplore – direct incitement, but marginalize and denigrate Jews through religious, philosophical and/or pseudo-scientific arguments (e.g. Max Scheler, Kevin McDonald). They will also offer cover or support for the less-educated, more overt kind of anti-Semites when circumstances require.

Consider the case of Cardinal Michael von Faulhaber (1869–1952), the leader of Germany's Catholic community, who is a hero to many Catholics for having repudiated the Nazis' claim that the Old Testament is irrelevant or antithetical to Christianity. He did this in his Advent Sermon in Munich, 1933, the year Hitler seized power and burned the Reichstag to the ground. At the same time, however, Cardinal von

Faulhaber rebuked German Jews for lacking loyalty and roots, on the one hand, and spiritual substance on the other. Guenther Lewy observes that:

> Cardinal Faulhaber's Advent sermons in 1933, in particular, are remembered for their eloquent vindication of the sacred character of the scriptures of the Old Testament. But Faulhaber went out of his way to make clear that he was not concerned with defending his Jewish contemporaries. "We must distinguish," he told the faithful, "between the people of Israel before the death of Christ, who were vehicles of divine revelation, and the Jews after the death of Christ, who have become restless wanderers over the earth. But even the Jewish people of ancient times could not justly claim credit for the wisdom of the Old Testament. So unique were these laws that one was bound to say: 'People of Israel, this did not grow in your own garden of your own planting. This condemnation of usurious land-grabbing, this war against the oppression of the farmer by debt, this prohibition of usury, is not the product of your spirit.'"
>
> (Cited in Voegelin, 1999, p. 190)

"... not the product of your spirit". Quite a damning indictment, isn't it? On the one hand, Faulhaber defended the Old Testament's continuous and unceasing relevance to the Catholic faith. On the other hand, he denigrated the authors of that text and their lineal descendants, who are ostensibly even *less* deserving than their ancient forebears, who were already deemed spiritually deficient. Moreover, Faulhaber's claim that after the crucifixion of Jesus, Jews became "restless wanderers over the earth" implies that we wandered freely, of our own accord, presumably because we lack a strong sense of loyalty or attachment to a people or a place. Did Jews sometimes sail to other shores in search of opportunities denied them in their countries of origin? Yes, of course they did. In this respect they are no different from immigrants of all faiths and nationalities. But the *mass* migrations of Jews across Europe, North Africa and the Middle East over the last two millennia were seldom voluntary. The headlong flight of Jews from the Iberian peninsula during the Spanish (and Portuguese) Inquisition is merely the best known example of this kind of treatment, where nearly 200,000 Jews were compelled to leave their homes because of vicious persecution, not for lack of loyalty or because of a spontaneous inclination to wander.

The second, more serious reproach in Faulhaber's sermon is the claim that even *before* the death of Jesus, Jews lacked the spiritual substance to claim credit for the "wisdom of the Old Testament", and therefore to generate the prohibitions on "usurious land grabbing" contained, one assumes, in Law of the Jubilee, or the Deuteronomic Code, as it is sometimes called. Nonsense! The Hebrew Bible – or the Old Testament, as Christians call it – was originally written in paleo-Hebrew, Hebrew and Aramaic. Moreover, the "unique" laws that Faulhaber commended were introduced by Ezra and Nehemia sometime after the fall of the Babylonian empire in 539 BCE, when roughly 40,000 Jews then in exile where finally permitted to return to their ancestral lands to rebuild their Temple (Ledowitz and Taylor, 1999).

I call attention to Faulhaber's remarks because the same reproaches – that Jews are deficient in roots, spirituality and a sense of justice – were invoked to explain their rejection of Jesus' claim to be the Messiah, and to justify the charge that Jews are chiefly or solely responsible for his crucifixion. A sublimated or secularized version of this reproach resurfaced in Jung's milieu in the interwar period when, as Geoffrey Cocks observed, fascists:

> ... capitalized on a more general cultural movement against materialism that often caricatured Jews as lacking "spirituality". Historian George Mosse has shown how pervasive this caricature was, citing as one example the late 19th century Swiss historian Jacob Burkhardt, who, while not close to the nascent *völkisch* movement, fulminated against the decline of ... civilization as evidenced by the machinations, among others, of venal Jews.
>
> (Cocks, 1989, p. 164)

Unlike Hitler – a low-brow/high-intensity anti-Semite – Burkhardt was a high-brow/low-intensity anti-Semite (Sherry, 2010, Chapter 2). Likewise with Faulhaber. He never incited German Catholics to commit violence against Jews directly. He merely provided them with the perfect justification for passivity and indifference to their fate, encouraging a bystander mentality, and giving the Nazis latitude to pursue their goals without hindrance from Catholic believers.

Of course, this crude classification of modern anti-Semites – (low-brow/high-intensity versus high-brow/low-intensity; religious versus racial, etc.) – is by no means exhaustive. There were always plenty of low-brow/low-intensity anti-Semites who were just somewhat prejudiced against Jews, and high-brow/high-intensity anti-Semites like Ezra Pound or Martin Heidegger, for example. Moreover, there are instances when the boundaries between religious and racist anti-Semitism are extremely blurry (e.g. Father Charles Coughlin). The point of contrasting low-brow/high-intensity anti-Semites with their high-brow/low-intensity counterparts is to establish that in politically volatile environments, these two varieties– the semi-literate and the highly educated – often collaborate in various ways; that the latter may provide a measure of cover and legitimacy for the former, even if they deplore (or claim to deplore) the violence their more vitriolic counterparts deploy to "cleanse" the world of Jews.

Sacred history and cultural identity: Jews and Christians

If you set aside the fact-free, quasi-delusional character of anti-Semitic *chimeria*, the strangest thing about anti-Semitism in the West is that it even exists in the first place. After all, Judaism and Christianity share a great deal in common. For example, when we address the Almighty in prayer, Jews and Christians alike address God as our Creator, as our Judge or as our Redeemer. According to tradition, all living creatures owe our existence to God. The beauty and the mystery of the world are all His creation, His handiwork, which we can never hope to match, or even to fathom fully. Rabbi Abraham Joshua Heschel (1907–1972) identified the attitude evoked by this concept of God as *awe* (Heschel, 1955). Considered as our final Judge, the God of the Bible evokes more mixed feelings – feelings of guilt and fear, but also of confidence that if we strive to be just and merciful, or to emulate God in our conduct with our fellow creatures, we will be loved and honored, at least by Him. Why? Because the God of the Bible is a great equalizer. On the Day of Judgment, we are told, God is completely indifferent to our worldly status or accomplishments. God's omniscience permits him to see into the inner recesses of our hearts, to discern our real thoughts and hidden motives, and to ignore any misunderstandings and misconceptions that others still harbor after we pass on. He will treat us justly, even if our fellow creatures have not done so during our lifetimes. So the prospect of standing naked before God on the Day of Judgment can strike fear in our hearts. But it can also inspire hope of vindication and forgiveness, especially – though by no means only – if we suffer for His sake.

Our feelings and beliefs about God as cosmic Judge are closely aligned to feelings and beliefs about God as our Redeemer, or liberator. God liberates us from idolatry and belief in false gods who cannot save us, and if we are currently enslaved or brought low by the malice or indifference of our oppressors, faith in God will sustain us spiritually so that we can endure, and keep our hope and our dignity intact, despite all, until we are finally free.

But the resemblance does not end here. Because of the Biblical depiction of God the Creator, Jews and Christians share the conviction that each and every human being is made in the image and likeness of God. The practical upshot of this belief is our shared emphasis on the oneness or unity of the human family, on the one hand, and on the worth and singularity of each and every human being on the other. In addition, Judaism and Christianity converge impressively in their emphasis on the virtues of justice and mercy, and their desire to foster a truth-loving disposition among the faithful. These core values – justice, mercy and a truth loving disposition – are emphasized repeatedly in the Hebrew Bible, but nowhere as often or as emphatically as they are in the Prophetic literature.

Why all the venom directed toward Jews, then, if Judaism and Christianity share these core convictions? And why do they share them in the first place? In all likelihood, Judaism and Christianity share these beliefs and values because they were rooted in the religious environment that Jesus grew up in, Cardinal Faulhaber notwithstanding. Many Christians find this proposition hard to believe, if not profoundly insulting, because they were taught in early childhood that Jesus first taught or inspired this kind of faith in God, while Jews of that era were supposedly lacking in these beliefs and sensibilities, being robotically enslaved to "the law".

Given how deeply the beliefs and values of Jewish and Christian believers converge on certain issues, atheists and rationalists may be forgiven for wondering why the two groups can't just get along, or for characterizing the conflicts between them as little more than "the narcissism of minor differences". But Freud himself observed that the narcissism of minor differences is fertile ground for conflict among peoples who actually share a great deal in common, and whether these differences are major or minor is really a matter of perspective (Freud, 1930).

In any case, Freud and Jung both laid considerable emphasis on the differences between Jews and Christians – or in Jung's case, for the most part, between Jews and Aryans – for different reasons and in different ways. Freud came of age in a world teeming with anti-Semitic sentiments and stereotypes (Schorske, 1981; Frosh, 2005), and felt called to defend his people's honor by exaggerating the differences between the Jews and their Christian adversaries and detractors. And as we shall see presently, Jung emphasized their differences because of his racist sympathies and leanings, and because he was deeply offended by Freud's charge that he was indeed an anti-Semite.

So on reflection, the rupture between Freud and Jung and its painful and prolonged aftermath were both profoundly shaped by the ways in which Freud and Jung experienced and addressed anti-Semitism in 20th century European culture and politics. Obviously, ancestral loyalties played a role on both sides. But neither Freud nor Jung were "believers" in a conventional sense, much less theologians. So before we launch into a discussion of their relationship, and the ways in which their personal, theoretical and political differences were constellated by their attitudes toward Jews and Judaism, we need to address the theological differences between Jews and Christians more deeply to assess whether (or to what extent) they were merely secularized or "sublimated" into the history and politics of the psychoanalytic movement, and to what extent other cultural conditions or personal complexes and rivalries shaped the early history of psychoanalysis.

Theologically speaking, one very important difference between Jews and Christians is that when we address Him as our Creator, Judge or Redeemer, Jews are always talking about one and the same Being – the One who ultimately confers our personhood on us. Christian theology is quite different in this respect, since it posits (and insists upon) a division of labor among the various roles and functions that God presumably performs. In Christianity, as in Judaism, God the Father is always considered the Creator. But Jesus, who is God's Son (in the Christian faith) is depicted as our Redeemer. As a result, in Christianity, God the Redeemer, namely God the Son, is equated with second Isaiah's suffering servant. In Judaism, by contrast, the suffering servant merely represents the Jewish people in exile after the destruction of the First Temple, not the Messiah, who in truth is not actually our Redeemer, but merely our Redeemer's earthly representative.

So, unlike Jewish theology, which pivots entirely around God the Father, Christianity has a Trinitarian theology. (Islam, based upon the Koran, resembles Judaism more than Christianity in this respect.) Some devout Christians find these differences quite troubling, grounds for worry or reproach. Others take them in stride, presumably because the structures of piety and devotion attached to the Jewish depiction of God as Creator, Judge and Redeemer clearly prefigure the piety of their Christian counterparts.

Among the first to discern the deeper sources of conflict between Jews and Christians was Rabbi Arthur Hertzberg (1921–2006), a prominent leader of the American Jewish community. Like Rabbi Heschel, Rabbi Hertzberg participated in some of the first rounds of Jewish–Catholic dialogue during the second Vatican Council from 1962 to 1965. Twenty years later, Hertzberg published an article entitled "Christian-Jewish Relations: '*Nostra Aetate*' Twenty Years On" in *The Christian Science Monitor.* He noted the enormous progress in Jewish–Christian dialogue in the intervening years, but cautioned that the limits of dialogue were fast approaching, or had already been reached, saying that both parties would likely be disappointed by their counterparts in years to come. Why? Commenting on *Nostra Aetate*, and the Church's *Declaration of 1974*, Hertzberg pointed out that

> From the Catholic perspective, Judaism must be respected because it is part of the religious history of Christianity. To be sure ... the Church (now) condemns any undue pressure for conversion and ... respects those who are committed to the first Biblical revelation. What is between the lines of these Catholic documents – and what has appeared again and again at discussion tables between leaders of the two faiths – has been the profound desire (I would even say need) of Catholics to have Jews agree that Jesus is part of their religious history and that Jewish theology must take of him no less seriously than Catholic theology takes account of the Patriarchs and the Revelation to Moses on Sinai. Every time I, for one (and I of course have not been alone) have said that Jesus is not more important to Judaism than Muhammad is to Christianity faces have fallen.
>
> In my view, Christianity at its deepest level continues to grapple with the problem of the rejection of the New Dispensation by Jews when it first appeared among them. Even liberal Catholics regard the renewed dialogue with Jews as an historic opportunity to solve this problem – that is, to make sense of what appears to Christians to be incomprehensible; that the people which best know Jesus ignored him when he appeared and continue to do so. In this expectation, the Catholics in dialogue with Jews will continue to be disappointed, and this despite the attempt to "solve" this problem through "two covenant" theology that was proposed by Franz Rosenzweig ...
>
> (Hertzberg, 1985, reprinted in Hertzberg, 1992, pp. 199–201)

Rabbi Hertzberg's reflections touch on the heart of the matter. But Hertzberg speaks of the "religious history" of the Jews. I prefer to speak of the *sacred histories* of Jews and Christians. The sacred history of Jews, of Christians or indeed any other religious community is tied closely to their interpretation of their sacred scriptures, and has very little relation to history proper. Granted, historical people and events figure in their narratives, and many orthodox and fundamentalist members of the faith in question stubbornly insist on the inerrancy of scripture, believing firmly in its historicity. But at the end of the day, real historians don't trade in supernatural entities or events, and with rare exceptions (e.g. Arnold Toynbee, Eric Voegelin) seldom expound on the meaning of Revelation, however conceived. Why? Because at the end of the day, a group's sacred history is the story it tells itself to explain to individual believers – and potential converts – the emergence or origins of the community, the nature of its relationship to God (and to other faith communities), the trials and triumphs that the group's ancestors endured or enjoyed, and their continuing relevance to believers in the present day. In short, sacred history is emblematic of a group's collective identity, its "being-for-itself". It is not accurate, impartial, balanced or even remotely comprehensive in its assessment of the available evidence or its elucidation of the facts. On the contrary, it is thoroughly tendentious, and probably has to be, to insure the cultural cohesion and continuity of the group in question.

So, to understand what is at stake here, please note that the sacred history of the Jews is punctuated by pivotal events – the Creation, the Flood, Abraham's covenant and journey into Canaan, the flight to Egypt, the Exodus, Sinai, the Temple, Babylonian exile and return, and so on, right up to the destruction of the Second Temple. Christians share this sacred history up to a point. But for the average Christian, the events that occur in the Hebrew Bible merely *prepare the way* for Jesus' Incarnation, and the Biblical episodes most pertinent to the Christian's faith are those that (allegedly) predict Jesus' birth and ministry, and the events his surrounding his trial, his crucifixion and resurrection. As a result, Christianity imbues believers with a very specific attitude toward history; one that Jews do not share. Christians believe that the sacrifice Jesus made to redeem humankind was a singular, salvific event; the single most important and consequential event in human history. That is why the death of Jesus is commonly referred to as "the Crucifixion". Christians believe that everything that occurred prior to the crucifixion of Jesus was chiefly prelude. Moreover, they insist that everything that happened *after* the death of Jesus must be interpreted in light of this event, which the philosopher Hegel aptly named "the hinge of history".

By contrast with the average Christian believer, Jews do not see the people or events chronicled in their scriptures as a prelude to a new Revelation. They note that in Jesus' lifetime, the Roman authorities governed Israel, Judea and Samaria with an iron fist, and crucified thousands of Jews between the time of Jesus' birth and the destruction of the Second Temple in 70 AD. As proof, they cite Titus Flavius Josephus (37–100 CE), author of *The Jewish War* – an historical treatise written in Greek for non-Jewish audiences. Josephus was born Yosef ben Matityahu, and led the Jewish forces against the Roman occupation in the Galilee until 67, when he surrendered to the Roman emperor Vespasian, and became his slave. Josephus recorded that three years after his surrender to Vespasian, the Romans strung up thousands of Jewish men, women and children to demoralize and punish the Jews, and that crosses lined the road to Jerusalem for many, many miles (Josephus, 1980). The Roman authorities did not censor or object to Josephus' harrowing account of the Jewish wars, no doubt because they believed that their genocidal campaign was thoroughly justified; indeed, a cause for considerable celebration. (See, e.g. The Triumphal Arch of Titus.) The upshot, however, is that Jews regard the death of Jesus not as a singular or pivotal event, but as one crucifixion among many, many others performed by the Roman authorities. So though most Jews freely acknowledge that Jesus' death was a tragic occurrence, they hold the Roman authorities, rather than their own forbears, chiefly responsible for his death, and hasten to point out that thousands more met precisely the same fate as he did. So *the* crucifixion, as Christians call it, was and remains merely *a* crucifixion, from the Jewish point of view. Even now, it remains quite difficult for Jews engaged in earnest dialogue to broach this subject with their Christian counterparts, even tactfully, without running the risk of giving offense. Why? Because at the end of the day, the Jew's steadfast refusal to credit the singularity or the salvific nature Jesus' crucifixion feels like an insult, an attack on the very the foundations of Christian belief.

So as Hertzberg intuited, even if Jews and Christians understand one another perfectly, sooner or later, a measure of mutual disappointment will inevitably ensue. Christians must reconcile themselves to the fact that Jews welcome their friendship, and respect and understand their theological frames of reference. But at the end of the day, they cannot possibly share it (especially with reference to Jesus' crucifixion, and to the many doctrinal ramifications that follow from this) without abandoning their own ancestral faith. Similarly, Jews must be reconciled to the fact that even when Christians regard most Jews with kindness and respect, or as equal citizens and allies, really devout Christians will probably always regard Jews as somewhat obstinate and incomplete, as proto-Christians or para-Christians or Christians in waiting; in other words, as somehow "lesser than" their Christian counterparts, who enjoy the full measure of God's grace. So, as long as Jews are Jews, and Christians are Christians, they must agree to disagree on this matter. All that remains to those still engaged in dialogue is to decide whether to haggle over our different versions of scared history, or to stress the beliefs and values we nevertheless share in common as a basis for solidarity and mutual respect.

But while the lines of cleavage between Jews and Christians are crystal clear in retrospect, they were anything but clear to the Roman ruling class in the first century. And no wonder! The first community of worshippers who believed that Jesus is the Messiah were led by Jesus' brother James (or Jacob), who was originally a Pharisee. They spoke Aramaic and prayed in Hebrew, as Jesus had. They thought of themselves as Jews, and were nonetheless obliged to observe all the Jewish Holy Days and festivals, to be circumcised (if male), and to keep the Jewish dietary laws, too. They also rejected the divinity of Jesus, and belief in the Virgin Birth. Unlike James, who did not attempt to convert non-Jews to his community, St. Peter encouraged gentiles to join, and declared that only those born to Jewish parents need be circumcised and remain observant Jews. Gentiles were free of such obligations. The next major Christian leader, St. Paul, went further, and actually forbade anyone who believed in Jesus from observing Jewish rituals and festivals, even if they were born Jewish. He argued that Jesus' teaching had completely superseded the older, Mosaic covenant, reducing the parent faith to the status of idolatry. Not only did Paul dismiss traditional Jewish observance as idolatrous, he introduced the concepts of Original Sin and the Holy Trinity, and helped insure that the New Testament was written in Greek, rather than in Aramaic or Hebrew (White, 2004).

In all likelihood, Paul's agenda was twofold. On the one hand, by distancing himself from Judaism in this fashion, he sought to avoid the Romans' wrath against the Jews. Indeed, he preached unwavering obedience to Roman authority, rather than the stiff resistance that the Jews had offered them in the first century, which prompted the destruction of the Second Temple and the forcible removal of Jews from Jerusalem, and the thousands upon thousands of crucifixions that are *not* mentioned in the New Testament. On the other hand, by abolishing the rite of circumcision and traditional Jewish observances, and switching from Hebrew to Greek, he hoped to gain more pagan converts, and to gain a numerical advantage over the (increasingly hostile) Jewish communities that dotted the Mediterranean basin.

Paul's religious reforms were remarkably successful. In time, Christianity lost the stigma of its origins, becoming the official religion of the Roman Empire (White, 2004). Constantine the Great ruled the empire from 306 to 377 CE, and convened the First Nicene Council in 325, which produced the Nicene creed. He declared Sunday a day of rest for all citizens, and introduced the Julian or solar calendar to Christian communities, who had been using the Jewish or lunar calendar up until then. From that point onwards, many Christian Holy Days were timed to coincide with older, pagan festivals. But he removed the images of pagan gods from the coin of the realm, replacing them with Christian symbols, and forbade Jews from seeking converts, giving Christian missionaries the upper hand. Christianity took full advantage of this opportunity and soon spread to every corner of the Roman Empire (White, 2004; Lacquer, 2006).

Things went mostly downhill from there, from a specifically Jewish point of view. As James Carroll correctly points out, with rare exceptions, Christian priests, theologians and philosophers seldom incited believers to violence. But they almost always described and addressed the Jewish people derisively, as enemies or a pariah people who deserved to be shunned, scorned and confined to ghettos. Many large Jewish communities in Germany were ravaged and decimating during the Crusades (1095–1271).

Meanwhile, on March 31, 1492 their majesties King Ferdinand II and Queen Isabella I of Spain produced the Alhambra Declaration, which decreed that all Jews must leave Spain by July 31 of that year. The expulsion was the pet project of a Dominican friar named Tomas de Torquemada (1420–1498), the leader of the Spanish Inquisition, which was established by Ferdinand and Isabella in 1478 to ferret out and punish heretics, resulting in imprisonment and death for hundreds of innocent Jews, many of whom were burned alive.

Four years after the Alhambra Declaration, the King of Portugal issued a similar declaration. Jews fleeing the Iberian Peninsula often fled south to the Maghreb, or North Africa, or Eastward the Ottoman Empire, or North toward Holland – perhaps the only European country that accepted them at the time. It is also interesting to note that in the same month that Ferdinand and Isabella issued the Alhambra Declaration, they commissioned a *converso* (or Jewish convert) named Christopher Columbus to sail for the Indies, making Columbus the first Jew – and the first European – to set foot in the Western hemisphere. Nevertheless, the Spanish Inquisition was not formally abolished until 1840, and the ban on Jews living in Spain was not lifted until 1968.

As it turns out, Martin Luther (1463–1546) objected to the Spanish Inquisition, albeit briefly. In a pamphlet entitled *That Jesus Christ was Born A Jew*, published in 1523, Luther roundly criticized the Catholic Church, saying:

> Indeed, they treat Jews as dogs and not as humans, and all their discourse was to rebuke them and rob them of their property. And when they baptized them they did not instruct them in the lore of Christianity or in the Christian way of life, but enslaved them to the papacy and the clergy ... I hope that they will treat the Jews well, and if they lead them calmly through Scripture, many of them will become honest Christians and return to their ancestors,

to the faith of the Prophets and the Patriarchs ... If the Apostles, who were also Jews, had approached us, the gentiles, as we, the gentiles, approached the Jews, not one gentile would have become a Christian. Since they approached us, the gentiles, as brothers, we too should treat the Jews as brothers so that we should be able to convert them ...

So initially, Luther explained the refusal of Jews to convert to Christianity as the result of ill treatment at the hands of brutal clergymen and a perfectly sensible loathing for the Papacy; of wariness toward the pagan elements that had gradually intruded on Christian worship – above all, the cult of the Virgin, which he despised. Luther even deluded himself into thinking that once he had purged Christianity of these sordid accretions, Jews would convert *en masse*. However, after two decades, Jews still rejected his overtures, and he finally condemned them as "Children of Satan, condemned to perdition", and in 1543, exhorted his contemporaries as follows:

First, to set fire to their synagogues or schools.

Second, I advise that their houses also be razed and destroyed.

Third, I advise that all their prayer books and Talmudic writings, in which such adultery, lies, cursing and blasphemy are taught, be taken from them.

Fourth, I advise that their rabbis be forbidden to teach henceforth on pain of loss of life and limb.

Fifth, I advise that safe-conduct on the highways be abolished completely for Jews.

Sixth, I advise that ... all cash and treasure of silver and gold be taken from them.

Seventh ... Let whomsoever can, throw brimstone and pitch upon them, so much the better ... and if this be not enough, let them be driven like mad dogs from the land.

(cited in Berke, 1996, p. 345)

This inflammatory speech was not an isolated incident. Luther's last sermon, delivered three days before his death, was another attack upon the Jews. Surely this signifies something. Indeed, it is instructive to note that *Kristallnacht*, a vicious Nazi pogrom in 1938, was timed to occur on November 9–10 to coincide with Luther's birthday. Moreover, Luther's utterances were often read in Protestant Churches during the Nazi era to incite and legitimate the various abuses that culminated in the Holocaust. And as Jung pointed out in *Aion*, many members of the Nazi elite persuaded themselves that they were merely "finishing Luther's work" (Jung, 1959, p. 102).

Jews generally fared better in Calvinist milieus than in Lutheran ones. John Calvin (1509–1564) was more kindly disposed toward Jews than Luther, believing that some were actually destined for election despite their non-Christian beliefs. His French followers, the Huguenots, were persecuted fiercely by the Catholic Church, and were far more respectful of Jewish beliefs and practices. In the 20th century, they were even accused by some Catholic leaders of conspiring with Jews and Freemasons to undermine the French monarchy, and many risked their lives to aid Jews who were hiding from the Nazis in occupied France. Holland, a predominantly Calvinist country, welcomed Jews fleeing the Spanish Inquisition, and the City of Amsterdam accorded them equal rights as citizens in 1595 – long before any other state or municipality would. There is also a deep and direct connection between C.G. Jung and the Swiss Evangelical Reformed Church, centered in Basel. Jung's father Paul (1842–1896) and his maternal grandfather, Samuel Preiswerk (1799–1871), were both Calvinist ministers, and both accomplished scholars of Biblical Hebrew and Old Testament studies. Preiswerk, in particular, was known for advocating forcefully for the return of Jews to Ottoman ruled Palestine, and the creation of a Jewish state. He was, in short, a "Christian Zionist", whose memory and ideas were invoked by none other than Theodor Herzl at the first Zionist congress in Basel on August 31, 1897.

Sacred history and cultural identity: Jews and Muslims

Thus far, we've addressed the sacred histories and divergent interpretations of scripture found in the Judaism and Christianity. But what of Judaism and Islam? Is anti-Semitism in the Muslim world rooted in theological differences like these? Yes and no. Jews and Christians clash over their interpretation of Biblical texts, but Muslims follow the Koran, a text composed by the Prophet Mohammad (570–632) over a period of 23 (lunar) years. In consists of 114 surahs, ranging from 3 to 286 verses in length.

While undoubtedly a text of great beauty (Arberry, 1996), parts of the Koran are devoted to confounding and contesting the sacred histories of both Jews and Christians. For example, in Mohammed's retelling of the Exodus from Egypt, Mohammed places a character named Haman, whom the Book of Esther identifies a minister in the court of the Persian King Ahasuerus, in the court of the (nameless) Pharaoh who allegedly obstructed the departure of the Hebrew slaves under Moses' leadership; a man who, if he ever actually existed, lived roughly 1,000 years later, and in a land more than 2,000 kilometers away from this nameless Pharaoh's court. In his retelling of the life of Jesus, Mohammed credits the miracle of the Virgin Birth, but denies that Jesus was the Son of God, or was even actually crucified, thereby invalidating a central tenet of the Christian faith, and depriving Christians of their core rationale for persecuting Jews. Moreover, the Koran contains frequent exhortations to believers to reject a Trinitarian concept of the Deity.

Like Jews, who believe that righteous gentiles have a share in the afterlife and the Resurrection, despite the fact that they are not Jewish, Mohammed claimed that a small minority of Jews and Christians would be saved on the Day of Judgment. This startling concession appeared to imply a sense of kinship with members of the earlier Abrahamic faiths. However, Mohammed still consigned the majority of Jews and Christians to Gehenna (Hell), and in surah five, entitled *The Table*, Mohammad declares:

> O believers, take not Jews and Christians as friends; they are friends of one another. Whoso of you makes them his friends is one of them. God guides not the hearts of the evildoers.
>
> (Arberry, 1996, p. 136)

Still, though he frequently lumps Jews and Christians together, many of Mohammed's angriest denunciations are directed specifically at Jews. Mohammed writes:

> O Messenger, let them not grieve thee that vie with one another in unbelief, such men as say with their mouths: "We believe" but their hearts believe not. And the Jews, who listen to falsehood, listen to other folk, who have not come to thee, perverting words from their meanings ... Those are they whose hearts God desired not to purify; for them is degradation in this world; and in the world to come awaits them a mighty chastisement
>
> (Arberry, 1996, p. 134)

Further below, in the same surah, Mohammed admonishes the Jews, saying that "Whomsoever God has cursed, and with whom He is wroth, and made some of them apes and swine ...", implying that many Jews are bestial, less than human. And he repeatedly reproaches Jews for being treacherous and deceitful, for rejecting or murdering their own prophets, just as Christian anti-Semites did. Granted, if this were an isolated outburst, confined to a single surah, it would not justify the suspicion that Mohammed was an anti-Semite. But there are dozens of passages in other surahs just as vehement as this one; passages that depict Jews as an actual or potential threat to the well-being of their non-Jewish neighbors.[1]

According to some scholars of the Koran, the earlier surahs, written in Mecca, express a more positive attitude toward Jews than the later ones, which were written in Medina. According to others, there is no discernable shift, and the Prophet was consistent throughout (Lacquer, 2006). What is not disputed, however, is that Mohammed, a merchant, competed fiercely with two powerful Jewish clans for control of access to the Silk Roads (and therefore much lucrative trade) while the Koran was being written, and that he waged violent campaigns against them: once in Medina in 625, and again in Khaybar in 628. In the end, he successfully wrested control of the trade routes from his Jewish competitors.

On reflection, Mohammed's animus toward Jews was doubtless influenced by the fact that the Jews of Arabia refused to recognize him as a Divine Messenger, and probably scoffed at his retelling of Hebrew scriptures. What the Koran does not address specifically is that Mohammed and his followers were also in sharp economic conflict with them. Clearly, Mohammed wished to nullify their economic power by subduing them militarily, rendering it difficult to disentangle his military, political and economic objectives from his religious motives, and consequently, from the meaning(s) of the term *jihad* in Muslim circles today. But once the Jews were vanquished, and assigned a permanent subordinate status as dhimmis[2] by Mohammed and his successors, Jews were no longer experienced as powerful adversaries, a role increasingly assigned to Christians. As a result, Muslim anti-Semitism subsided somewhat, and Jews generally fared better in Muslim lands than they did in Christendom, right up until the late 18th century. Indeed, in some places, Jewish communities actually flourished in the Muslim world.

That said, it is not the case that Muslim anti-Semitism then vanished abruptly, only to erupt belatedly as a response to Zionist aggression. Jews were not universally accepted and protected by their Muslim rulers, as some apologists would have us believe. The correspondence of Rabbi Moses Maimondes (1146–1204) attests to the anguish and suffering of Jews living in Spain and North Africa in his lifetime (and afterwards). Maimonides fled his native Cordoba because of intense persecution by the Almohad dynasty, who abolished the Jews' traditional dhimmi status and forced them to convert, die or flee, much like the Spanish

Inquisition did more than two centuries later. Closer to our time, the novels, memoirs, essays and books of Albert Memmi (1920–2020), a Tunisian Jew, give eloquent expression to the suffering of the Jews of Tunis, who had settled there before the arrival of the first Christians, never mind the first Muslims, but were treated with cruelty and contempt by their Muslim neighbors and rulers.

However, it is true that Muslim anti-Semitism, which never abated entirely, was profoundly exacerbated by the Balfour Declaration, the Zionist movement and the creation of the State of Israel. As a result, as we shall see further below, Islamism – a fundamentalist strain of Islam that is vehemently anti-Semitic – often lumps all Jews with Western colonizers and imperialists, whom they refer to contemptuously as "Crusaders". The irony entailed in suggesting that Jews are "Crusaders" or allies of Crusaders is not lost on those familiar with Jewish history. The tiny kernel of truth embedded in this absurd epithet is that, at its inception, the Zionist movement embraced progressive European values that baffled and antagonized the Muslim inhabitants of Palestine and Muslims around the world, which prompted a fierce backlash. But these ideas and ideals were obviously *not* the same ones that prompted medieval Christians to massacre Muslims *and* Jews for the sake of defeating "the infidel".

Notes

1 Here please note the claim made by many Palestinian activists and promoters of the Boycott, Divest and Sanction movement that Arabs, being Semites, cannot possibly be anti-Semites; that the term "Arab anti-Semitism" is simply a non-sequitur. This clever but disingenuous argument flies in the face of mountains of historical evidence, but does call attention to the somewhat inexact meaning of term "anti-Semitism". That is why we defined this term (in Chapter 1) more in keeping with the original meaning of the term, which is equivalent to the older German term "Judenhasse" – Jew hatred.

2 Dhimmi is an Arabic word meaning a "subjugated person", i.e. someone who is not Muslim, and therefore not subject to Sharia law. Dhimmis are governed by their own religious laws, e.g. Halakah, in the case of Jews, but must pay a special tax for their community's protection by the local authority. Their testimony against Muslims was inadmissible as evidence in a court of Sharia law, they were forbidden to carry weapons, ride horses or camels, and their religious practices and places of worship were severely circumscribed. Dhimmi status was originally extended to Jews, Christians and Sabeans, and later extended to Zoroastarians, Hindus and Buddhists.

References

Arberry, A.J. translator. 1996. *The Koran Interpreted.* New York: Simon and Schuster.

Berke, J. 1996. "The Wellsprings of Fascism: Individual Malice, Group Hatreds and the Emergence of National Narcissism." *Free Associations* 6, no. 3, pp.334–50.

Bronner, S. 2020. "Conspiracy Fetishism, Community and the Anti-Semitic Imaginary." *Antisemitism Studies* Vol. 4, Issue 2 (Fall, 2020); Trans. *Una Citta* nr.261 (November 2019), 43–46. http://antisemitismstudies.com/index.html

Burston, D. 2014. "Anti-Semitism", in *The Encyclopedia of Critical Psychology*, ed. Thomas Teo, New York: Springer.

Carroll, J. 2001. *Constantine's Sword.* Boston: Houghton Mifflin.

Cocks, G. 1989. "The Nazis and C.G.Jung", in Maidenbaum, A. and Martin, S. *Lingering Shadows: Freudians, Jungians and anti-Semitism.* New York: Shamabala.

Cohn, N. 1996. *Warrant for Genocide: The Myth of the Jewish World Conspiracy and the Protocols of the Elders of Zion.* London: Serif.

Crossan, J.D. 1996. *Who Killed Jesus? Exposing the Roots of Anti-Semitism in the Gospel Story of the Death of Jesus.* San Francisco: Harper.

Freud, S. 1930. *Civilization and Its Discontents.* Vol. 21, Standard Edition, London: Hogarth Press.

Frosh, S. 2005. *Hate and the "Jewish Science": Anti-Semitism, Nazism and Psychoanalysis.* New York: Palgrave MacMillan.

Hertzberg, A. 1992. *Jewish Polemics.* New York: Columbia University Press.

Heschel, A. J. 1955. *The Prophets: An Introduction.* New York: Harper and Row.

Josephus, 1980. *The Jewish War.* Trans. G.A. Williamson. New York: Penguin Books.

Jung, C.G. 1959. *Aion: Researches into the Phenomenology of the Self* (R. F. C. Hull, Trans.). Princeton, NJ: Princeton University Press.

Lacquer, W. 2006. *The Changing Face of Anti-Semitism.* New York: Oxford University Press.

Langmuir, G. 1990. *History, Religion and Anti-Semitism.* Berkeley: University of California Press.

Ledowitz, B. and Taylor, R. 1997. "The Law of Jubilee in Modern Perspective". *Vermont Law Review*, 22 (1), pp. 157–172.

Ruether, R. 1997. *Faith and Fratricide: The Theological Roots of Anti-Semitism.* Eugene, OR: WIPF & Stock.

Schorske, C. 1981. *Fin-de-Siécle Vienna: Politics and Culture.* New York: Random House.

Sherry, J. 2010. *C.G.Jung: Avant-Garde Conservative.* Cham, Switzerland: Palgrave MacMillen.

Smith, D. 1996. "The Social Construction of Enemies: Jews and the Representation of Evil." *Sociological Theory* 14, no. 3, pp. 203–240.

Voegelin, E. 1999. *Hitler and the Germans*. Columbia: University of Missouri Press.

White, M.L. 2004. *From Jesus to Christianity*. San Francisco: Harper Collins.

Williamson, A. 1989. "The Cultural Foundations of Racial Religion and anti-Semitism." In Maidenbaum, A. and Martin, S. *Lingering Shadows: Freudians, Jungians and anti-Semitism*. New York: Shamabala.

2 Enlightenment, emancipation and the birth of Zionism

The French Enlightenment

After the Reformation, the development that reshaped European politics and culture most was the Age of Enlightenment, which began with the death of Louis the 14th in 1721, and culminated in the publication of Denis Diderot's *Encyclopedia*, which appeared in a series of volumes issued between 1751 and 1772. Collectively, the philosophers of the Enlightenment posed an even greater challenge to the Christian view of sacred history than either Judaism or Islam had. Why? Medieval Christians held that all believers are equal in God's eyes, in the sense that each and every human being is created in the image of God, and therefore capable of achieving salvation in the afterlife, provided that they confess Jesus as their Savior, of course. But that is as far as their belief in equality went. As far as *this* world goes, medieval Christians thought that it was sinful to violate or breach the feudal hierarchy. As a result, you had one system of rights and of legal penalties for commoners, peasants and tradesmen, and another one entirely for the aristocracy. In such a climate, there could be no rationale for the civic emancipation of Jews. Their treatment as second or third class citizens was simply a given, since they were not even part of the community of believers.

Moreover, from the medieval standpoint individuals may or may not make progress in their moral or spiritual growth, or in their relationship with God. But that is an individual, not a societal affair. The idea of collective human emancipation, fostered by the growth of literacy and the dissemination of reason, would have struck them as ridiculous, if not sacrilegious. Why? Because according to Scripture, ever since the Fall, humankind is enmeshed in a world of suffering and woe, and attempts to improve our earthly condition through "works" (or our own worldly efforts) distract us from our true spiritual vocation. Our main task in life is to merit salvation to that we can experience God's grace and enjoy eternal bliss in the afterlife. This emphasis on *otherworldly* salvation, and the tendency to denigrate efforts to change or improve our earthly condition, would have rendered most medieval Christians skeptical, if not downright hostile of any modern notion of progress.

Enter the Marquis de Condorcet (1743–1794), an Enlightenment philosopher who said that there is a natural *telos* or end-goal to human history; one which leads to the gradual improvement of the whole world. Indeed, as the 18th century drew to a close, Condorcet depicted this historical trend, which he called "Progress" as a slow but inexorable and gradually accelerating process that started in Europe, and would eventually encompass the whole planet, liberating even the most backward and superstitious corners of the globe. Condorcet believed that the dissemination of scientific knowledge through public education and the Enlightened reform of government and law would eventually produce a universal world order based on reason and tolerance, and which would confer undreamed of moral and material blessings on ordinary people, bringing peace, prosperity and brotherhood to all (Bronner, 2004).

Critics and supporters of the Enlightenment have both noted that Condorcet's idea of progress, on which most modern notions of progress are modelled, is rooted in a kind of secularized Messianism, in which the era of universal brotherhood, peace and prosperity arrives, not by divine intervention, but through the growth of reason, science and technology. And it was for that reason that it was rejected by many pious souls – Jewish, Christian and Muslim – well into the 20th century. Why? Because the God of Abraham, Isaac and Jacob, and by extension of Jesus and Mohammed, is our Creator, Judge and Redeemer, on whom all earthly blessings depend. But the Enlightenment argued to the contrary that *our salvation in this world depends primarily upon the development of our own reason*, and our ability to understand and harness nature's forces *without our even having to pray*. Even when it was not actively hostile to organized religion, Enlightenment thought encouraged self-reliance and laxness of religious of observance, and a focus on this world, rather than the next.

So, to put the issue bluntly, deeply religious Jews and Christians were often quite offended by the secular Messianism of the Enlightenment, which they construed as a form of idolatry, or collective self-worship. Jews had an additional reason to mistrust the Enlightenment. Leading figures like Voltaire and Diderot were bitterly anti-Semitic, and held Jewish culture and civilization in even deeper contempt than they did the Catholic faith. Nevertheless, it is thanks to the Enlightenment that the normative ideal of *equality* became an integral feature of our political discourse, and in the long run, this benefited Jews (Lacquer, 2006).

Anyway, because of the Enlightenment, the emergence of equality as a normative ideal for political life was closely associated with the idea of progress, and exerted a strong pull on Jewish communities in Western Europe and North America all through the eighteenth, nineteenth and twentieth centuries. Why? Because progress promised to bestow religious tolerance and a generally brighter future on those who embraced it, enabling Jews to imagine a future in which their present reality was transformed, and they could live without fear and without reproach in the same civic universe as non-Jews. So, while many orthodox Rabbis were fiercely opposed to the dangers of modernism and secularism, and shunned the blandishments of science, materialism and technology, many Jews embraced progressive causes of one kind or another.

Even so, equality came slowly, and did not erase or even subdue anti-Semitism appreciably for long. After the French Revolution, in 1789, the French National Assembly was debating the Declaration of the Rights of Man and Citizen to decide whether universal human rights applied to Protestants and Jews. Finally, they decided to extend citizenship to Jews, but only on condition that they renounce their Jewishness, or at any rate, set it aside in civil society. Even so, emancipation came slowly – 1790 for Sephardic Jews, 1791 for Ashkenazim. But full citizenship was revoked temporarily under Napoleon, and only fully restored again under King Louis XVIII in 1814 (Lacquer, 2006).

The Jewish Enlightenment and assimilation: from Mendelssohn to Dreyfus

The Jewish reaction to emancipation in France was mixed. The prospect of comingling with Christians as equals was quite intoxicating to some Jews, but quite threatening to others, who feared that assimilation would inevitably ensue. And so, by the early 19th century, a deepening split emerged in Europe's isolated and formerly cohesive Jewish communities – a split between orthodox traditionalists who clung to the old ways, and modernist Jews who followed Moses Mendelssohn (1729–1786), the leader of the Jewish Enlightenment, or the *Haskalah*. Mendelssohn was the son of a Torah scribe from Dessau – an autodidact who rose from obscurity and crushing poverty to become one the leading philosophers in Germany after Leibniz. He was widely admired among non-Jews for the profundity of his thought and his sparkling German prose. Mendelssohn translated the Hebrew Bible into German in 1783, in the hope and expectation that Jews who spoke Yiddish, for the most part, would now read and converse fluently in German, which he believed would be the language of Jewish emancipation. In addition, he started a movement which promoted the modernization of Jewish education to promote their full participation in civic life; which prefigured many ideas of Reform Judaism. As a result, Jews who had formerly had a very narrow religious education began to study secular subjects, and became deeply versed in the works of Lessing, Goethe and Kant – among others. They also started to publish, get jobs and play a vigorous role in German (and Austrian) academic life (Elon, 2002).

While Mendelssohn had many followers, however, many Jews *resisted* the Haskalah's educational program, arguing that Mendelsohnn's efforts to modernize Judaism would lead inevitably to secularism, assimilation and the loss of a distinctive Jewish identity. And perhaps they were right. Mendelssohn never wavered in his loyalty to Judaism. But of his six children, only his eldest son, Joseph, retained the Jewish faith. The rest – including, Abraham, the father of Felix Mendelssohn (1809–1847), who composed The Reformation Symphony – converted to Christianity.

Felix Mendelsohnn, Moses' grandson, is of particular interest here because he was vilified by Richard Wagner (1813–1883) in a scurrilous pamphlet entitled "Judaism in Music" (1850), which signaled the arrival of a racist–essentialist variant of anti-Semitism; one that vigorously discouraged conversion to Christianity, and saw Jewishness as a hereditary taint, something carried in the blood, which poses a potential threat to "pure" Christian/Aryan peoples through intermarriage or "race mixing". Wagner's son-in-law, Houston Stewart Chamberlain (1855–1927), a favorite of Adolf Hitler's, popularized this paranoid and incendiary brand of anti-Semitism in *The Foundations of the Nineteenth Century* (1899). Chamberlain also promulgated the myth of an Aryan Jesus and was often dubbed "Hitler's John the Baptist" (Elon, 2002).

Another example of racial anti-Semitism was the case of Heinrich Heine (1797–1856), a lawyer who became a famous dramatist, poet and satirist, and was widely admired by "non-Jewish Jews" like Marx and Freud. Heine was born in Düsseldorf to Jewish parents who were not observant. Düsseldorf was under French occupation from the time of his birth until 1815, so he spent his formative years under French influence, which permitted Jews to participate fully in civil society and the professions. Later on, the Prussian government restored severe restrictions on the Jewish community, so he converted to Lutheranism in 1825 as "the ticket for admission to European culture".

Heine was a gifted poet, a brilliant satirist, and on the whole, a decent human being. But he did not possess a shred of piety, Jewish, Christian or otherwise, so his motives for conversion were purely secular; the desire to avoid discrimination and Jew-baiting. Lacking the consolations of faith, however, he soon regretted his decision to convert, because as he later discovered, his decision did little or nothing to deter the anti-Semitic taunts and abuse directed at him by critics as he became more famous and successful (Elon, 2002).

An even more distressing situation confronted a non-observant French Jew named Alfred Dreyfus (1859–1935), who was catapulted to fame because of the scandal surrounding his unjust imprisonment. Dreyfus was born in Mulhouse in the Alsace region. As a young man, he attended the military academy at Fountainbleu, and in 1889, was made a Captain. In 1891, he was admitted to the Superior War College, graduating ninth in class. Given his ability, he should have risen through the ranks, but in 1892, General Bonnefond, who was in charge of the College, arbitrarily lowered his test scores (and those of another Jew, Lieutenant Picard) on the grounds that "Jews are not wanted" among the higher ranks. Dreyfus protested, but to no avail. Indeed, his efforts to rectify this injustice were bitterly resented by his superiors and were used against him later.

In 1894, Dreyfus was arrested and charged with giving military secrets to the Germans. The charge was baseless, the evidence against him flimsy and contrived, but Dreyfus was condemned, court-martialed and sent to Devil's Island in 1895. The Army and the Church, which were typically at odds in the 19th century, both condemned Dreyfus and all Jews for their lack of loyalty to *la patrie*, and a fresh wave of anti-Semitic hatred swept through France, fed by a zealous Catholic press. One notable exception was the journalist and novelist Émile Zola (1840–1902), who reviewed the details of the Dreyfus' case thoroughly, and pressed privately for a re-trial before he spoke out publicly. When efforts to retry or repeal Dreyfus' sentence failed, in 1898, Zola published an open letter to President Felix Faure that condemned the entire military elite for a grotesque miscarriage of justice.

Zola's bold letter, "J'Accuse ...", created a huge international outcry. As a result, Zola was convicted of libel and fled to England. In 1899, however, he was officially pardoned, and returned to France to continue the fight to clear Dreyfus' name and restore the honor of the Republic. Dreyfus was also pardoned in 1899, then released from Devil's Island, but his status as a pardoned prisoner carried with it a presumption of prior wrong-doing and prevented him from serving in the Army again. The lingering stigma remained in effect until 1906, when the real traitor was publicly identified. As it transpired – and as Zola had suspected – the Army brass had known who the real culprit was all along, but to save his reputation, and to spare themselves from shame and embarrassment, they blamed the Jew (Lacquer, 2006).

In retrospect, it is clear that the Army's choice of scapegoat was wildly popular because the vast majority of people *wanted* to believe in Jewish guilt. Why? For medieval Christians, as Nietzsche observed, Jews were rather like the Chandala or "untouchable" caste of India – people at the very bottom of the social pyramid, who should never attempt to rise above their station. From this point of view, a middle class Jewish professional – whether in business, law or the military – would *always* be an anomaly, who came by his prosperity in some sneaky or unscrupulous way. From this point of view, *any* effort by Jews to normalize their lives and to join the mainstream were an affront to the laws of God or nature.

One journalist who covered the Dreyfus case was a contemporary of Freud's, one who lived several blocks away from him, named Theodor Herzl. Before he tried his hand at journalism, Herzl had trained as a lawyer, and was therefore well versed in rules of evidence and legal procedures. Herzl had become the Paris correspondent for the *Neue Freie Presse*, a prestigious Viennese daily in 1891, the same year Dreyfuss was promoted to the rank of Captain. Although Herzl had been reluctantly coming to the conclusion for some time, the Dreyfus case demonstrated to him the absolute impossibility of assimilation, and the dire necessity of creating a Jewish homeland. So in 1896, one year after Dreyfus was incarcerated on Devil's island, Herzl published a book called *The Jewish State*, and convened the first Zionist congress in Basel, one year later, in 1897. From that point onwards, Herzl devoted the rest of his life to the Zionist cause.

Capitalism, socialism and Zionism

Mendelssohn, Heine and Dreyfus were three highly accomplished individuals who are still remembered today because they had many admirers and defenders among the non-Jewish population. But the vast majority of Jews who suffered similar persecution were completely without allies or recourse when they received similar treatment. Even so, 19th-century anti-Semitism was already a somewhat different beast than its medieval precursor. There was a new racist strain, already present at mid-century, in Wagner's repulsive rivalry with Mendelssohn. And while medieval Christian anti-Semitism was rooted mostly in theological differences – and much as old, medieval prejudices were revived and rehearsed during the Dreyfuss affair – there were other, specifically economic factors that contributed to the astonishing resurgence of anti-Semitic hatred in late 19th century.

Remember, France was still an overwhelmingly Catholic country, and a small number of wealthier Jews were now an integral part of a growing system of international trade and finance that was gradually undermining the Church's waning influence in France and in Europe as a whole. As a result, the Catholic Church vigorously opposed to the processes of secularization and modernization that the Enlightenment opened up for Jews, because the Church was – and for the most part, still is – a thoroughly feudal institution. Feudalism was rigidly hierarchical, and the rate of technological innovation in feudal times was extremely slow, being modulated by custom and tradition. Capitalism, by contrast, thrives on ceaseless technological innovation and market forces that create considerable upward and downward social mobility, disturbing the stable feudal hierarchy, and creating vast new industrial enterprises and urban areas.

Meanwhile, most Jewish inhabitants of these bustling cities lacked the education and opportunities of their middle-class counterparts, and gravitated toward socialism and trade unionism to promote and defend their interests. They often rejected the nationalism that their more prosperous cousins typically embraced in favor of an internationalist perspective. Like all members of the working class, poorer Jews had to curtail their education to work in factories and sweat shops – often in their early teens. This drastically curtailed their educational opportunities. The trade union movement provided semi-literate adults with the only education they were ever likely to receive. In fact, socialists and trade unionists made a concerted push to promote adult learning and literacy in Europe, the United Kingdom and the United States, and the Jewish workers who came into their orbit – especially those fleeing Eastern Europe, where conditions grew increasingly harsh after 1880 – were increasingly drawn toward progressive politics and causes (Howe, 2005).

Unlike their bourgeois counterparts, who made inroads in business, the professions and academia, Jewish socialists and trade unionists were suspicious of nationalistic movements and ideals. People like these tended to think internationally and believed that emancipation for the Jews is dependent on the emancipation of the entire working class. Some of them became Marxists, and followed Marx's prescription for Jewish emancipation, which was essentially a kind of cultural self-erasure, a rejection of their heritage, and total immersion in the class struggle. Another group of Jewish socialists, known as the Bund, believed that Jews that must express their solidarity with the international working class while maintaining a vibrant (though thoroughly secular) cultural life. Whereas Moses Mendelssohn imagined that German was the language of Jewish emancipation, the Bund (which discouraged assimilation) promoted the growth of Yiddish-based cultural institutions – schools, theaters, charitable societies, sporting leagues – in Europe and America. They were not particularly religious, and felt no need to create a Jewish homeland per se, believing that anti-Semitism was a tool of capitalist oppression, and would vanish eventually when socialism was achieved (Brossat and Klingsberg, 2016).

Meanwhile, however, many Jews despaired of *ever* being accepted in non-Jewish society, even among the working class, and believed that the creation of a separate Jewish homeland was a vital precondition for Jewish emancipation. However, despite agreement on this score, the Zionist movement was never a homogeneous entity. It took shape primarily through an unlikely coalition of middle and working class Ashkenazim, or Jews of European backgrounds, but was intended to benefit all Jews, including these from Sephardic, Mahgrebi and Mizrahi backgrounds, who spoke Ladino and Arabic, respectively. That is why Zionists made a Shephardic dialect of Hebrew their *lingua franca*, rather than privileging German, Yiddish, Ladino or any of the other languages spoken in the diaspora.

The early Zionists drew inspiration from various sources, including Moses (Moritz) Hess (1812–1875), the French philosopher who "converted" Friedrich Engels, and then Karl Marx, to the socialist cause in 1843. Hess was a member of the International Working Men's Association from 1840 to 1860, but broke with Marx and Engels in 1845. They, in turn, attacked him viciously in *The Communist Manifesto* (1848), claiming that Hess' socialism was based on a doomed attempt to realize certain ethical ideals – those of universal human dignity and freedom – rather than a program of "scientific socialism" based on an "objective" understanding of economic and historical conditions. They referred to Hess derisively as "the communist Rabbi", because he maintained that the Deuteronomic Code or the Law of the Jubilee was an early prescription for agrarian socialism (Avineri, 1981).

By the end of the 1850s, Marx and Engels had seized complete control of the International Working Men's Association, and a deeply demoralized Hess left Paris for Cologne, where he was alarmed by the recent ground-swell of anti-Semitism coursing through Europe. He did not abandon his socialist aspirations or ideals, but felt called upon to assert the legitimate aspirations of his people, and so published a book called *Jerusalem and Rome* in 1862, which was read and admired by Theodor Herzl, who greeted Hess as his spiritual preceptor. Hess' concept of a Jewish homeland was a model democracy that shunned the excesses and crushing poverty of life under industrial capitalism. Hess' book fostered the growth of Labor Zionism and the kibbutz movement in Israel.[1] Though he died in Paris, his remains were eventually moved to the Kinneret cemetery, interred alongside Socialist-Zionists such as Ber Borochov, Nachman Syrkin and Berl Katznelson (Avineri, 1981).

Another source of inspiration was the American poet Emma Lazarus, who was also deeply involved with the trade union movement and New York's growing Jewish community on the lower East Side of Manhattan. She called for the creation of a Jewish homeland in Palestine in 1884, more than a decade before Herzl convened the first international Zionist congress in Basel. The word "Zionism" had not yet been coined, so we should probably describe her and Moses Hess as Zionist precursors, or "proto-Zionists". But that is a secondary issue. What matters here is that her call for the creation of a Jewish home-land alienated many orthodox and Reform Jews living in the United States. The orthodox Jews complained that unless or until the Messiah arrived, any attempt to orchestrate a return to Zion betokened a lack of faith in God. Reform Jews argued that Lazarus' proto-Zionist stance betokened a lack of faith in America itself, and urged Jews to dem-onstrate their devotion to their adoptive homeland, rather than to a distant land governed by the Ottoman Empire. The American Jewish Committee – a powerful lobby group – actually maintained a hostile stance toward Zionism until 1947, when Britain, which had received a mandate to replace the Turks after WWI, announced plans to partition Palestine.

And so, on reflection, it is important to note that not all Jews are Zionists. On the contrary, many orthodox Jews, Reform Jews and Bundists actively opposed the Zionist movement before and, to a much lesser extent, after WWII. Even so, the list of non-Zionist (or anti-Zionist) Jewish intellectuals includes many notable figures, including Hermann Cohen, Franz Rosenzweig, Hannah Arendt, Erich Fromm, Tony Judt, Joel Kovel, George Steiner and Noam Chomsky, among others. But by the same token, not all Zionists are Jews. Jung's maternal grandfather, Samuel Prieswerk, was merely one in a long line of Protestant clergymen (dating all the way back to the 17th century) who called for the Restoration of Jews to the Holy Land. Christian Zionists (or "Restorationists") in England included Sir Isaac Newton, Oliver Cromwell, Anthony Ashley-Cooper, the 7th Earl of Shaftesbury, George Eliot, Lord Balfour, David Lloyd George, Winston Churchill and W.H.Auden . Prominent Christian Zionists in the United States included Presidents John Adams and Woodrow Wilson, Professor George Bush of New York University (and forbear of both Presidents Bush), the Rev. Martin Luther King, Jr., and the late, great Johnny Cash and his wife, June Carter Cash, as well as countless conservative, Right-wing evangelists with anti-Semitic leanings, like Billy Graham, Jerry Falwell, Pat Robertson, whose support of Israel is rooted in the conviction that Jews are unwittingly hastening the second coming of Jesus and the mass conversion of the Jews.

That being so, it is extremely important not to conflate or confound the categories of Judaism, or Jewishness, and Zionism. The former refer to religious belief or ethnicity, the latter to a political stance shared by many, but not by all Jews. Now that we've covered the preliminaries, setting the stage for what follows, our task is to demonstrate the relevance of the preceding to understanding Jung's relationship to Jews and Judaism, to Freud and his followers, and the accusations of anti-Semitism that dogged Jung for much of his career.

Psychoanalysis, politics and anti-Semitism

The first point to consider here is that, in several important ways, Freud was a child of the Enlightenment. His Enlightenment sympathies are evidenced in his militant atheism and anti-clericalism, and his belief that reason, and reason alone, can mitigate (though not eliminate) mental and emotional suffering. By contrast, Jung was a conservative Romantic whose sympathies, for the most part, ran in precisely the opposite direction (Sherry, 2010). This may not have been apparent to either of them when they began their collaboration, but Jung made this abundantly clear on October 1, 1939, eight days after Freud died, and precisely one month after Hitler's invasion of Poland. Writing in the Sunday edition of the *Basler Nachrichten*, Jung said that

> Freud's psychology moves within the narrow confines of nineteenth century scientific materialism. Its philosophical premises were never examined, thanks obviously to the Master's insufficient philosophical equipment.
>
> (Jung, 1939 p. 47)

Despite (and perhaps because of) these limitations, Jung went on to say,

> Freud
> ... wanted to unmask as illusion what the "absurd superstition" of the past took be a devilish incubus ... and ... reduce him to a "psychological formula." He believed in the power of the intellect; no Faustian shudderings tempered the hubris of his undertaking ...

He expected enlightenment to do everything-his favorite quotation was Voltaire's "Écrasez l'infâme".

(Jung, 1939, p. 48)

Jung then went on to insist that

Ludwig Klages saying that "the intellect is the adversary of the soul" might serve as a cautionary motto for the way Freud approached the possessed psyche ...

Freud's "psychological formula" is only an apparent substitute for the daemonically vital thing that causes a neurosis. In reality, only the spirit can cast out "spirits" – not the intellect, which is at best a mere assistant, like Faust's Wagner, and scarcely fitted to play the role of an exorcist.

(Jung, 1939, pp. 48–49)

Clearly, Jung had little patience for Freud's Enlightenment leanings. Moreover, it should be noted, he wasn't alone in this respect. In "The Mind of a Rationalist: German Reactions to Psychoanalysis in the Weimar Republic and Beyond", Anthony Kauders points out that many of Jung's contemporaries, including Hans Prinzhorn, Wilhelm Salewski, Arthur Kronfeld, Edgar Michaëlis, Oswald Bumke, Alfred Hoche and Rudolph Allers, expressed similar objections (Kauders, 2005). Jung, however, had an additional trait worth mentioning – a deep affinity for the medieval tradition of demonological conjectures that preceded the Enlightenment perspective on mental disorder. He indicated as much by saying that Freud could not provide a cure for neurosis, because he was "scarcely fitted to play the role of an exorcist" – the tacit implication being that Jung himself was eminently qualified to do so, perhaps courtesy of his "personality number two".

At the same time, and indeed, in the very same essay, Jung praised Freud as a "great destroyer", noting that the turn of the century "offered so many opportunities for debunking that not even Nietzsche was enough". Jung continued:

Freud completed the task, very thoroughly indeed. He aroused a wholesome mistrust in people and thereby sharpened their sense of real values. All that gush about man's innate goodness after the dogma of original sin was no longer understood, was blown to the winds by Freud, and the little that remains will, let us hope, be driven out for good and all by the barbarism of the twentieth century. Freud was no prophet, but he is a prophetic figure. Like Nietzsche, he overthrew the gigantic idols of our day, and it remains to be seen whether our highest values are so real that their glitter is not extinguished in the Acherontian flood.

(Jung, 1939, pp. 46–47)

By situating Freud in the same "debunking" tradition as Nietzsche, Jung put his finger on the elements of Freud's work that run counter to the Enlightenment's glib, optimistic philosophy of history. After all, Freud believed in progress. But it was progress with a hefty price tag attached; progress at the expense of happiness and peace. No matter how much we change or improve our material circumstances, said Freud, we human beings are doomed to experience inner and inter-personal conflict, because our basic instincts require ever more domestication and refinement with the steady advance of culture, rendering all of us "enemies of civilization" in our unconscious. Moreover, much as he cherished Enlightenment rationalism and materialism, after WWI, Freud's outlook became notably gloomier, and he never ruled out a possible return to barbarism. Indeed, he would not have written *Civilization and Its Discontents* if he had not feared its imminent arrival on his doorstep. In this Jung and he agreed; though when Jung wrote this ambivalent appraisal of his erstwhile friend and collaborator in September 1939, the barbarians were no longer merely on the doorstep. They were already sacking the house, preparing to burn it to the ground.

Another point to be born in mind, going forward, is that Freud and his followers saw Jung as an accomplice to the barbarism that was sweeping Europe, which threatened to annihilate the Jewish people altogether. And they were not alone in this, either. This state of affairs, which started brewing during WWI, prompted angry accusations and recriminations between Freud and Jung and their respective followers, spawning a vast literature that is still growing today. This prompts the question: Was Jung actually an anti-Semite, as Freud and his followers alleged? Many of Jung's apologists insisted he was not, implying that the Freudian faithful simply misunderstood or willfully misconstrued Jung's utterances, actions and intentions in the thirties, possibly with malicious intent. However, that response is also overly simplistic. Ultimately, once they've seen the evidence, readers must decide for themselves whether, or to what extent, the polemical exchanges on either side were justified by the evidence at hand, and what implications all this may has for the history of psychoanalysis and depth psychology and its relevance to today.

Note

1 A kibbutz is an agrarian community where differences in wealth are minimal or non-existent, and where the means of production – land, herds, factories and so on – are owned in common, and profits distributed equally among members. Kibbutzim – which is plural for kibbutz – are affiliated through loose networks, but each one is a free-standing, autonomous entity – an open, face-to-face participatory democracy where every adult has a vote, and men and women are completely equal.

References

Avineri, S. 1981. *The Making of Modern Zionism*. New York. Basic Books.

Bronner, S. 2004. *Reclaiming the Enlightenment. Toward a Politics of Radical Engagement*. New York: Columbia University Press.

Brossat, A. and Klingberg, S. 2016. *Revolutionary Yiddishland: A History of Jewish Radicalism*. Translated by David Fernbach. London: Verso.

Elon, A. 2002. *The Pity of It All: A History of the Jews in Germany 1743–1933*. New York: Picador.

Howe, I. 2005. *World of Our Fathers: The Journey of East European Jews to America and the Life They Found and Made*. New York: New York University Press.

Jung, C.G. 1939. "In Memory of Sigmund Freud." Reprinted in *The Spirit in Man, Art and Literature*, translated R.F.C. Hull, Bollingen Series XX. Princeton, NJ: Princeton University Press, 1971.

Kauders, A. 2005. "The Mind of a Rationalist: German Reactions to Freud in the Weimar Republic and Beyond." *The History of Psychology* 8, no. 3, pp. 255–270.

Lacquer, W. 2006. *The Changing Face of Anti-Semitism*. New York: Oxford University Press.

Sherry, J. 2010. *Carl Jung: Avant-Garde Conservative*. London: Palgrave MacMillan.

3 Jung, Freud and the "Aryan unconscious"

A botched succession

C.G. Jung was the only son of Emilie Prieswerk and a Swiss Reformed Pastor named Paul Jung; a man widely known as an Old Testament scholar, whose dissertation at the University of Göttingen was on the Arabic version of the *Song of Songs*. Jung's father died of cancer in 1897, a year after Jung had commenced his university career, a tragedy which precipitated a financial crisis for him and his mother. Nevertheless, he completed his medical studies in Basel three years later, and became the assistant to Professor Eugen Bleuler at the Burghölzli Clinic in Zürich from 1899 until 1909, when he opened up a private practice in nearby Küsnacht. Bleuler introduced Jung to Freud's writings around 1904, and in 1905, Freud obtained a copy of Jung's *Diagnostic Association Studies*, which he keenly admired, prompting Jung to initiate a correspondence with Freud in 1906. This soon led to their first face-to-face meeting in Freud's home in Vienna in 1907, during which the two men spoke at length, for a full fourteen hours!

The two men got on famously for a time. The trouble started two years later, perhaps, on March 25, 1909, when Jung was visiting Freud in Vienna, when Freud tried to enlist Jung to take on a larger leadership role in the psychoanalytic world. In the course of the same evening, Freud and Jung had an earnest discussion about occult phenomena. As Jung later recalled:

> Because of his materialistic prejudice, he rejected this entire complex of questions as nonsensical, and did so in terms of so shallow a positivism that I had difficulty checking the sharp retort on the tip of my tongue.
>
> (Jung and Jaffé, 1962, p. 155)

While Jung managed to contain his temper, apparently, their conversation was interrupted by two mysterious explosions from the bookcases in Freud's study, which Jung described as "catalytic exteriorization phenomena", or poltergeists. According to Jung, Freud dismissed this suggestion as nonsense but was still quite rattled by the experience. So on April 2, 1909, Jung wrote to Freud from Zürich, saying that on his return home he was afflicted with *"sentiments d'incomplétude"*, and worried that his "spookery" had struck Freud as "altogether too stupid and unpleasant". And on April 16, 1909, Freud wrote back to say:

> It is strange that on the very same evening when I formally adopted you as eldest son, and anointed you – *in partibus infidelium* – as my successor and crown prince, you should have divested me of my paternal authority, which divesting seems to have given you as much pleasure as I, on the contrary, derived from the investiture of your person.
>
> (McGuire, 1974, p. 218)

Freud then went on to explain that he had heard these apparently inexplicable noises emanating from his bookcases several times since Jung's return to Zürich, deducing that they must therefore have a perfectly natural explanation, having nothing to do with Jung's thoughts, feelings or moods at that moment, adding that as a result "my credulity, or at least my willingness to believe, vanished with the magic of your personal presence". In short, said Freud, the whole business was a complete coincidence, although the pleasure Jung took in divesting Freud of his "paternal authority" – which would presumably include his authority to name Jung as his successor – was not.

This explanation of events probably did not sit well with Jung. After all, twelve years earlier, in 1897, in the Zofingia lectures he delivered to fellow medical students at the University of Basel, Jung championed the ideas of physicist Johann Zöllner (1834–1882), an avid spiritualist and anti-Semite who opposed Jewish emancipation and what he termed the "Judaization of science". In this same lecture, the young C.G. Jung had ridiculed the mechanistic materialism of Zöllner's bête noir, Emil du Bois Raymond (1818–1896), a German Jew who was one of Freud's mentors at the Vienna Institute of Neurology (Sherry, 2010).

In any case, a few months after the book-case episode, in January 1910, Freud wrote to Jung and proposed aligning the fledgling discipline of psychoanalysis with the Society for Ethical Culture, an organization that sought to place morality on a purely rational and secular basis, eschewing the supernatural altogether. On February 2, 1910, Jung scoffed at the idea, and shared his own vision of the future of psychoanalysis, saying:

> I think we must give it time to infiltrate into people from many centers to revivify among intellectuals a feeling for symbol and myth, ever so gently to transform Christ back into the soothsaying god of the vine, which he was, and in this way absorb those ecstatic instinctual forces of Christianity for the *one* purpose of making the cult and sacred myth what they once were – a drunken feast of joy where man regained the ethos and holiness of an animal. That was the beauty and the purpose of classical religion, which from God knows what temporary biological need has turned into a Misery Institute. Yet what infinite rapture and wantonness lie dormant in our religion, waiting to be led back to their true destination! A genuine and proper ethical development cannot abandon Christianity, but must grow up within it, must bring to fruition its hymn of love, the agony and ecstasy over the dying and resurrected God, the mystic power of the wine, the awesome anthropophagy of the Lasts Supper – only this *ethical* development can serve the vital forces of religion.
>
> (McGuire, 1974 p. 136)

Perhaps the book-case episode was sheer coincidence. But this epistolary outburst was a shot across the bow. After all, Freud was inordinately fond of cigars, but he had no fondness for drink, or drinkers; something that Jung was well aware of. Also instructive is the fact that Jung referred to Christianity unabashedly as "our religion", ignoring Freud's Jewishness, implying in the process that unless or until Freud himself had a dramatic change of heart, he would never attain "the holiness and ethos of an animal" – something Freud would not have wanted, anyway. Finally, by depicting Christ as a belated avatar of Dionysus, and evoking the pagan imagery of a dying and resurrected God – which runs completely antithetical to Jewish teaching, of course – Jung effectively sidelined the historical Jesus, who was born and died a Jew, implying that we must look for our salvation to the pagan elements of Christianity that Freud found most problematic, and most likely to foster anti-Semitic feelings, as we shall see.

Despite these worrisome signs, on March 30, 1910, to the great dismay of his Viennese followers, Freud appointed Jung as the first President of the International Psychoanalytic Association (IPA); a position he held from 1910 to 1913. To justify his decision to his (mostly

Jewish) followers, Freud said that having a Christian psychiatrist at the helm would dispel the widespread impression that psychoanalysis is merely a "Jewish Science", hopefully blunting some of the anti-Semitic prejudice that his theories were likely to engender.

However, tensions between Freud and Jung escalated sharply shortly after Jung was appointed President of the IPA. Indeed, in October and November 1911, Emma Jung (1882–1955) even wrote privately to Freud, trying to ameliorate the growing tensions between her husband and him. While their brief correspondence ended on a cordial note, the tensions between Jung and Freud resumed swiftly on December 11, 1911, when Freud reported his impressions of Sabina Spielrein's recent presentation to the Vienna Psychoanalytic Association to Jung. Spielrein (1885–1942) was a former patient of Jung's from the Burghölzli, who studied medicine in Zürich from 1905 to 1911. Her presentation to the Vienna Psychoanalytic Society on December 10, 1911 attempted to synthesize and reconcile some of Jung's theories about the unconscious with Freud's own. Freud was not pleased, and he let Jung know it, too (Burston, 1994).

Things went downhill from there. All through 1912, Freud and Jung sparred over their theoretical differences in their correspondence – quietly at first, but with increasing vehemence and then with no holds barred by the year's end. By December 1912, it was abundantly clear to all concerned that Jung was not suited to play the role of Joshua to Freud's Moses; that Freud's fond fantasy of naming a non-Jewish successor to his "throne" was utterly misguided. During this same interval of time, Jung also became increasingly critical of Freud's leadership style, which Jung described as authoritarian, infantilizing and in the end, intolerable to anyone with an independent and creative spirit. At first, Jung was tactful enough to confine his misgivings about Freud's authoritarianism to their correspondence and conversations with members of his own inner circle. Freud, however, probably regretted his previous lapse of judgment, because he showed no such restraint. In a harsh, polemical essay called "On the History of the Psychoanalytic Movement", published in 1914, Freud said that, in the interests of furthering their friendship and collaboration, Jung had temporarily given up "certain race prejudices which he had so far permitted himself to indulge". The tacit implication of these remarks was that once their association dissolved, Jung reverted to his earlier, anti-Semitic stance.

German and Jewish psychologies: Jung contra Freud

Perhaps in response to this provocation, Jung started to publish papers which made unflattering comparisons between so-called "Jewish psychology" – epitomized in the theories of Freud and Adler – and Germanic or "Aryan psychology" as early as 1918. In these papers, Jung claimed that the "Jewish psychologies" of Freud and Adler reflected the contours and limitations of the Jewish psyche, but were not applicable to "Aryans". Remarks like these were few and far between for a decade or so, but increased noticeably in the late 1920s and early 1930s, and came to a sickening crescendo in a radio interview he gave to his pro-Nazi acolyte, Richard von Weizsacker, on May 26, 1933, where he characterized the theories of Freud and Adler as "corrosive" to the German psyche. As Richard Stein points out, the books of Freud and Adler had been publicly burned just two weeks earlier, and the adjective "corrosive" had become an integral feature of Nazi propaganda. Furthermore, Stein notes that:

> Jung went on to characterize the Jewish theorists as "hostile to life" – a phrase that more accurately described the Nazi repression, which he seemed tacitly to condone.
>
> (Stein, 1991 p. 100)

This dreadful event was followed by a paper entitled "On the Present Situation of Psychotherapy", published in March 1934, where Jung wrote the following. He said:

> If … I were to analyze Freud, I would be doing him a great and irreparable wrong if I did not take into account the historic reality of the nursery, the importance of emotional entanglements within the family chronicle, the bitterness and seriousness of early, acquired resentments and their compensatory concomitants of (unfortunately) unfulfillable fantasies … Doubtless, Freud means what he says, therefore he must be accepted as the person who says such things. Only then is his individual case accepted, and with him, are recognized those others whose psychology is similarly constituted. Now, insofar as one can hardly assume Freud and Adler are universally valid representatives of European humanity, there exists for myself the hope that I, too, possess a specific psychology and with me all those who similarly cannot subscribe to the primacy of the infantile-perverse wish fantasies or the urge to power.
>
> (Jung, cited in Harms, 1946/1991, p. 38)

At this point in his polemic, Jung was warming to his subject, preparing for a more forceful attack on Freud's credibility that would shortly follow. He said that if he were Freud's analyst, he would be bound to accept Freud's own theories as being valid for him and for "those others whose psychology is similarly constituted", namely, Jews. However, he hints that Freud would not accord Jung the same courtesy; that Freud would seek to impose his own theory on Jung. This is probably a belated and disguised complaint against the mistreatment he felt he experienced at Freud's hands. Jung then goes on to say:

> it has been a great mistake of all previous medical psychology to apply Jewish categories, which are not even binding for all Jews, indiscriminately to Christian Germans or Slavs. In so doing, medical psychology has declared the most precious secret of the German peoples – the creatively prophetic depths of soul – to be childishly banal morass, while for decades my warning voice has been suspected of anti-Semitism. The source of this suspicion was Freud. He did not know the Germanic soul any more than did all his Germanic imitators. Has the mighty apparition of National Socialism, which the whole world watched with astonished eyes, taught them something better? Where was the unheard of tension and energy when there was as yet no National Socialism? It lay hidden in the Germanic soul, in that profound depth which is every-thing else except the garbage bin of unreliable childish wishes and unresolved family resentments.
>
> (Jung, cited in Harms, 1946/1991, p. 38)

Jung makes an astonishing claim here, suggesting that up until recently, all "medical psychology" applied "Jewish" categories indis-criminately to Christian peoples. If true, this astonishing claim might have provided some slight justification for some of the comments that followed. But it was completely false, and one wonders what prompted Jung to confabulate so freely at this juncture. After all, Freud's ideas were never universally accepted by European psychiatrists during his lifetime. If they were, Freud would not have recruited Jung in the first place, nor given him such latitude, and struggled so mightily to keep Jung in the fold despite his follower's vocal misgivings, would he?

Nevertheless, Jung went on to claim that "Freud did not know the Germanic soul" which Jung insists is "everything except the garbage bin of unreliable childish wishes and unresolved family entanglements". And then, worst of all, Jung credits the Nazi movement with demon-strating the truth of this claim. The impression that Jung had a very personal score to settle with Freud are reinforced when Jung complains how often it happens that

otherwise serious physicians, in complete disregard of all fundamental tenets of scientific conscience, explain psychological material
by means of subjective conjectures – conjectures of which one can
really make nothing, except that they are attempts to find that particular obscene witticism through which the material under investigation could in some way be related to an anal, urethral or some
other sexual abnormality. The poison of devaluating interpretation
has infiltrated the very marrow of these people, so that they can no
longer think at all except in the infantile, perverse jargon of certain
cases of neuroses which are characterized by the special features of
Freudian psychology. It is really too grotesque that the physician
himself falls into that way of thinking that he rightly objects to as
infantile in others.

Jung continues

if the physician's thoughts overtly or silently are as negative and
devaluating as the patient's, and are equally desirous of pulling
everything into the infantile-perverse morass of an obscene wit-
psychology, one must not be surprised if the latter's soul becomes
a barren waste and he compensates for this barrenness by an incurable intellectualism.

(Jung, cited in Harms, 1946/1991, p. 40)

So, having vigorously rejected the charge of anti-Semitism, Jung
went on to state that Freud's soul is a "barren waste" comprised of
"an obscene wit psychology" and an "incurable intellectualism". Let's
be candid, shall we? This was tantamount to saying that Freud's ideas
about psychosexual development are completely irrelevant in most cases
of mental disorder, and that the effort to interpret clinical material in
light of these developmental schemata is really nothing more than the
product of a "dirty mind". Indeed, Jung's attack on Freud's "obscene
wit psychology" echoes the very same charges levelled at Freud by his
critics in 1906, when Jung had leapt to Freud's defense. Jung, who was
formerly Freud's champion, had reversed himself completely, siding
with Freud's adversaries from the turn of the century. Moreover, in this
same essay from 1934, Jung said that

Freud and Adler have seen very clearly the shadow which accom-
panies everyone. The Jews have this peculiarity in common with
women: Being physically weaker, they have to aim at the chinks in
their opponents armor, and since this technique has been enforced

on them during a history of many centuries, the Jews themselves are best covered at the spots where others are most vulnerable. In consequence of their more than twice as ancient culture they are vastly more conscious of human weaknesses and inferiorities and therefore much less vulnerable in this respect than we are ourselves.

(Harms, 1946/1991, p. 37)

And yet, in the very same paragraph as this statement, we find another statement, characterizing "the Jew" as

something of a nomad, never has produced and presumably will never produce a culture of his own, since all his instincts require a more or less civilized host nation to act as a host for their development

(Harms, 1946/1991, p. 37)

Before going further, let's tally up the attributes that Jung ascribes to the Jewish psyche. Echoing Otto Weininger, a notorious anti-Semite, Jung said that Jews resemble women because they are weaker than their (male) Aryan counterparts, but have a "more than twice as ancient culture" which bestows greater insight into people's psychological weak spots and vulnerabilities; traits developed in order to survive, presumably to compensate for their lack of physical strength and vitality.[1] Then, in the next breath, Jung asserted that Jews are nomads who lack any culture of their own because they require the hospitality of a "more or less civilized" nation to act as a "host". This parasitic mode of relatedness, like the Jew's weakness and his compensatory cleverness, presumably, are integral features of the Jewish psyche.

The attributes Jung bestowed on the Jewish people may seem a little odd, or even relatively harmless, and perhaps partially justified to some. So I hasten to point out that these same attributes are ascribed to Jews in Hitler's memoir, *Mein Kampf*. Granted, Jung's polemic is mercifully free of Hitler's lurid, chimerical fantasies about an international Jewish conspiracy that controls the media, the banks, the press and foreign governments, or his bizarre attempts to blame capitalism, communism, pornography, prostitution, the drug trade, jazz and modern art – in short, all the evils of modernity – on the Jews (Hitler, 1925). Jung wasn't stupid, after all. He even qualified his negative remarks by adding some positive traits, hinting that Jews, as individuals, are often more conscious and differentiated than their rustic Aryan counterparts.

As it turns out, Jung's suggestion that the average Jew is more conscious and differentiated was a backhanded compliment, because Jung believed that the seeds of cultural transformation and renewal reside in the as yet unrealized potential of the *collective* unconscious, and not in the sphere of individual self-consciousness. Moreover, this claim that "the Jew" is "something of a nomad" who lacks a culture of his own was published in 1934, when Nazis were telling Jewish citizens that they were not real Germans, but merely a "guest people", and therefore not entitled to the same rights and privileges as their Aryan counterparts, though many German Jews came from families that had settled the Rhineland in Roman times. And as we now know, this invidious rhetoric was merely a prelude to the Nuremberg Laws (1935), Kristallnacht (1938) and the Holocaust that ensued a few years later.

That being so, we are amply entitled to wonder: Did Jung crib these stereotypes from Hitler? No, not likely. Granted, the first volume of *Mein Kampf* appeared a decade before Jung's essay. But Hitler and Jung drew on same vocabulary of stock images and stereotypes that permeate the anti-Semitic imaginary of European nations to this very day. Though he was never a member of the Nazi party, like Martin Heidegger, Jung was quite well versed in the scurrilous, pseudo-scientific literature that justified anti-Semitic prejudice in the years leading up to WWII. And as Andrew Samuels points out, in 1934 – the same year he published "The Present Situation of Psychotherapy" – Jung and Matthias Göring co-signed a birthday greeting to Dr. Robert Sommer printed in the *Zentralblatt für Psychotherapie*, a journal of which Jung was the sole editor. Sommer was a cofounder of *The General Medical Society for Psychotherapy*, and was responsible for enlisting Jung to join their ranks, and becoming vice-President of this organization in 1930. Göring and Jung praised a book Sommer had written in, and lavished particularly fulsome praise on a chapter added in 1927, which traded in transparently racist tropes, affirmed that psychiatry is a branch of "raciology" and called for "selection of the gifted", i.e. eugenics.

The fact that Jung, the sole editor of this journal, offered warm birthday greetings to the author of these lines demonstrates that he was quite comfortable in the anti-Semitic milieu and thoroughly versed in their ideas about race and eugenics. Further evidence of his leanings in this direction are his collaboration with Jakob Wilhelm Hauer (1881–1962), the founder of the German Faith Movement, with whom he led seminars in Kundalini Yoga in 1932. The German Faith Movement was a neo-pagan organization founded in 1933 at Eisenach. It supported the Nazi party, rejecting Protestantism on the grounds that it was too infused with Jewish ideas and motifs. In the words of Hauer, the movement's founder: "… the German Faith Movement is an eruption from the biological and spiritual depths of the German nation", which is precisely how Jung construed the emergence of National Socialism in 1934 – as a prelude to spiritual rebirth and cultural consolidation, rather than a slide into barbarism (Sherry, 2010). As further evidence of this, consider his letter to Oskar Schmitz on May 26, 1923, where Jung says that Christianity, having emerged from a monotheistic religion is "wholly incongruous" with the pagan traditions that preceded it and that it is therefore:

> a grave error if we graft yet another foreign growth onto our already mutilated condition ... We cannot get beyond our present cultural level unless we received a powerful impetus from our roots. But we shall receive it only if we go back behind our cultural level, thus giving the suppressed primitive man in ourselves a chance to develop ... We must dig down into the primitive in us, for only out of the conflict between civilized man and the Germanic barbarian will there come what we need: a new experience of God.
>
> (Sherry, 2010, p. 71)

Anti-Semitism, "anti-Christianism" and neo-paganism

Before we delve further into this matter, we must put Jung and his circle on a back burner for the moment, and focus our attention on Freud's attitudes toward the Nazis and anti-Semitism. Freud's first attempt to explain anti-Semitism appeared in his case history on "Little Hans" (Freud, 1909), where Freud opined that anti-Semitism is the result of castration anxiety, which Freud claimed is universal. Given the overarching religious, historical and economic factors at play in the European psyche, which were addressed in Chapters 1 and 2, this explanation of anti-Semitism, which is all but forgotten, merits little or no discussion here. I merely mention it to demonstrate that the topic of anti-Semitism was already on Freud's mind, and that he felt that a psychoanalytic theory of this phenomenon was in order.

Freud never ceased believing that castration anxiety (and the rite of circumcision) potentiate anti-Semitic feelings among non-Jews. But in *Totem and Taboo*, published in 1913, Freud outlined an additional dimension to this theory; one with a more solid historical foundation. Following the French archeologist and religious historian Salomon Reinach (1852–1932), Freud contended that it was not Jesus, but Paul (Saul) of Tarsus who founded the Christian religion – a point on which most scholars are now in complete agreement. In the process, said Freud, St. Paul and his followers borrowed extensively from the mystery cults of pagan antiquity, substituting a mother-and-son oriented religion for the older, father-centered religion of the Jews, thus putting a new and decidedly Oedipal twist on the older, Jewish faith (Freud, 1914).

Freud revisited this thesis in his last book, *Moses and Monotheism*, where he further suggested that Christianity's concessions to paganism constituted a massive collective regression; one that marked a decisive shift *away from* Judaism, which had placed a complete ban on magic and superstition, and was therefore the more rational religion (Freud, 1939). This interpretation prompted Freud to conclude that Christian anti-Semitism arose from lingering pagan sympathies and inclinations that had been repressed since the advent of Christianity, and an unconscious hostility toward the Jews for inventing monotheism in the first place. And Freud was not alone in this. In *The Pillar of Fire*, Karl Stern recalled a conversation with a colleague at the German Research Institute for Psychiatry that took place in 1933. This young man was a follower of Wilhelm Hauer, but he had no reservations about dining with a Jew like Stern on occasion. Since seating in the cafeteria was usually segregated along racial lines, Stern was quite curious about this fellow, who told him:

> I used to be terribly anti-Semitic, you know, until I began to study the writings of Dr. Hauer. Then I found out that what we hate in Jews is not the Jews. It is Christ and the Christian religion. This religion is something so utterly alien to the very spirit of the European peoples that they revolt with their entire being against it. But although they feel revulsion they are not aware of its true origin. Hence that irrational hatred of Jews, because people vaguely feel that it is actually a Jewish way of feeling, thinking, acting, a Jewish norm of living that has been stuffed down their throats for the past two thousand years. Once you have found out that it is actually Christianity that is the painful foreign body in your flesh, something curious happens. You stop hating Jews. You regard them with the same kind of sympathy or antipathy that you might regard any other foreign nation.
>
> (Stern, 1951, p. 133)

Stern then wondered what features of Christianity were contrary to the European spirit. Echoing Jung's complaints to Freud about Christianity's transformation into a "misery institute", Stern's erstwhile colleague replied that Christianity imbued people with an unbearable sense of guilt. Then citing Tacitus' book *Germania*, he argued that Indo-Germanic people had a much higher idea of "the destiny of man", and even faulted Hitler for deflecting constructive anti-Christian sentiments into vulgar Jew baiting.

Was Karl Stern's cafeteria companion typical of Wilhelm Hauer's followers? Probably not. Most of them were ardent Nazis, and would never have consented to break bread with Stern. Even so, there is a striking similarity between Freud's theory of anti-Semitism and that of Stern's erstwhile colleague. They both contend that anti-Semitism is rooted in pagan sensibilities that rebel against the Judaic features of Christianity. Of course, their convergence on this matter does not alter the fact that Freud saw Nazis as a dangerous and regressive cultural force, and not as a (highly desirable) return to some authentically Aryan form of spirituality as Jung and Hauer did.

Though debatable, of course, Freud's claim that Judaism is a more rational religion than Christianity was widely shared by many Jews of that era; especially Jews who were strongly influenced by the spirit of the Enlightenment (Elon, 2002). Carl Schorske's masterful elucidation of the anti-Semitic currents that pulsed through Vienna as Freud came of age (Schorske, 1981) prompts the reflection that Freud's claims concerning the superior rationality of the Jewish faith were mostly a spirited rejoinder to stereotypes that marked the Jewish faith as inferior because lacking in genuine spirituality; a prejudice Jung shared evidently. (See below.) But even if Freud's theory were true, as Jung occasionally seems to concede, Jung and his followers never saw the rationalistic trend in 19th-century Judaism – which he dismissed along with Freud's "incurable intellectualism" – as a cause for celebration.

Another notable difference between Freud and Jung was that while Freud entertained several theories of anti-Semitism over the course of his career, Jung offered his followers none at all – not in print, anyway. However, he did remark that Jews, and in particular, Jewish intellectuals, brought anti-Semitic feelings on themselves because of their "anti-Christianism". He said this both before and after WWII. For example, in a letter to James Kirsch composed in May of 1934, Jung wrote:

> The Jewish Christ-complex ... makes for a somewhat hystericized general attitude ... which has become especially clear to me in the course of the present anti-Christian attacks upon myself. The mere fact that I speak of a difference between Jewish and Christian psychology suffices to allow anyone to voice the prejudice that I am an anti-Semite ... As you know, Freud previously accused me of anti-Semitism because I could not countenance his soulless materialism. The Jew truly solicits anti-Semitism with his readiness to

scent out anti-Semitism everywhere. I cannot see why the Jew, like any so-called Christian, is incapable of assuming that he is being personally criticized when one has an opinion of him. Why must it always be assumed that one wants to condemn the Jewish people?

(Lammers, 2011, p. 46)

In other words, said Jung, Jews are hypersensitive. Indeed, their irrational or excessive fears elicit the very reactions they dread from others, becoming a self-fulfilling prophecy. Similarly, in a letter to Mary Mellon dated September 24, 1945, Jung accused "Freudian Jews" in North America of starting the rumor that he was a Nazi. And along the same lines of his earlier letter, he now lamented the fact that

it is however difficult to mention the anti-Christianism of the Jews after the horrible things that happened in Germany. But Jews are not so damned innocent after all. The role played by the intellectual Jews in pre-war Germany would be an interesting object of investigation.

(ibid., p. 469)

The "horrible things that happened in Germany" is an obvious reference to the Holocaust, and once again, Jung's remarks suggest that the Jews are somehow responsible for their own misfortune, and that they attacked Jung, because of their own anti-Christian bias.

Meanwhile, in 1933, the year Hitler became Chancellor, Jung gave an interview on German national radio that raises all kinds of thorny questions. As Jay Sherry points out, when asked about the role of leadership in collective life, Jung told the German nation:

It is perfectly natural that a leader should stand at the head of an elite, which in earlier centuries was formed by the nobility. The nobility believe by the law of nature in the blood and exclusiveness of the race. Western Europe doesn't understand the specific psychic emergency of the young German nation because it does not find itself in the same situation either historically or psychologically.

(Sherry, 1991, p. 124)

Consider these comments carefully. First, Jung implies that the racist belief in "the blood and exclusiveness of the race" *is* rooted in natural law. This in turn appears to imply that the Nazi belief in racial "purity" and the superiority of Aryans is not merely intelligible, but justified. Then, somewhat later, he reproaches nations that greeted

Hitler's rise to power with such trepidation with misunderstanding "the young German nation" – as if Germany were "younger" than England, France or Poland. Can someone who spoke this way really disclaim any anti-Semitic feelings and sympathies? And if someone who speaks this way does not harbor anti-Semitic feelings, how can we account for an utterance like this, at a time like this, as anything other than an expression of complete insincerity or rank opportunism?

Another curious feature of Jung's complaints about Jews is that he associates their "anti-Christianism", as he called it, with a decidedly tribal mentality. In a letter to Erich Neumann dated April 27, 1935, Jung wrote that

> The Church is an ideal substitute for the chosenness of the people because it is spiritual, therefore universal, in contrast to the racial ties of the Jews ... The "tribal" national bonds with their secluded character seem to me – quite separately from their historical-psychological significance – to be a primitive relic, in comparison to the constantly evolving development of the Christian world of ideas, which only gives the impression of still being identical with the worldviews of early Christianity and which, in any case, was never a national bond, but from the very beginning, principally universal.
>
> (Jung, in Neumann, 2015, p. 21)

Like many of his Christian contemporaries then, Jung believed that Jews really are a distinct "race" with a grasping, materialistic and decidedly tribal disposition that is the opposite of the noble Christian ideal, which aspires to universality. Thus, Jung associated Judaism with tribalism, which he described as a "primitive relic" in comparison with "the Christian world of ideas" which is continually evolving, but rooted, in the first instance, in universalistic aspirations and ideals.

Though problematic in several ways, for the sake of argument, let's assume that Jung's analysis was correct. Even so, how do we square Jung's critique of Judaism with his take on National Socialism? Hitler believed that the German *völk* would achieve world-salvation through world-domination, and prized "racial purity" and exclusivity far more than the Jews ever did. Indeed, Nazi ideology was far more tribal, primitive and exclusive in its claims and aspirations than the Hebrew Bible. So why did Jung regard Jewish particularism to be evidence of spiritual stagnation, while the blatantly racist ideology of National Socialism was tolerated, if not welcomed, as evidence of an impending spiritual revival of world-historical dimensions, *especially* by a man who claimed to be Christian? (And if this isn't evidence of a double standard – one with ominous implications – what is?)

Nevertheless, most of Jung's Jewish followers vigorously defended him against the charge of anti-Semitism. They pointed out that Jung trained many Jewish analysts, including Erich Neumann, his close friend Gerhard Adler, Ernst Bernhard, Werner Engel, James and Hilde Kirsch, Heinz Westmann and Max Zeller (among others). Moreover, they argued that Jung used his influence in medical circles to help many Jewish physicians and their families to safety, and that he cultivated friendships with Rabbi Leo Baeck, the leader of Germany's Jews, and Baeck's protégé, Gershom Scholem, a kabbalistic scholar who became a frequent speaker at his Eranos conferences after the Holocaust. There is also the peculiar fact that after succumbing to a (second) heart attack in 1946, Jung had a vision in which he was nursed back to health by an elderly Jewish woman, who fed him kosher food, and that he was privileged to attend the wedding between "Malchut" and "Tifferet", two of the Kabbalistic Sephirot, or attributes of the Deity.

How do we make sense of these contradictory appraisals of Jung's attitude toward Jews, and the conflicting bodies of evidence on which they are based? Can they both be true? As it turns out, the answer is yes. That being so, the only way to reconcile these conflicting narratives is to acknowledge that Jung's attitude toward Jews was acutely ambivalent; that it contained strong philo-Semitic and anti-Semitic elements that waxed and waned as his circumstances changed (Drob, 2010). Evidently, then, Freud's accusation was not entirely wrong, merely one-sided.

Seven Sermons and *The Red Book*

Thus far, Jung's publications and occasional correspondence have furnished evidence of his ambivalent attitudes toward Jews. An additional source of evidence is the *Seven Sermons to the Dead*, a strange collection of fragments that Jung wrote in 1916 in his Black Book, and circulated privately among members of his inner circle. In it, he adopted the authorial persona of a second-century pagan Gnostic from Alexandria, a historical figure, named Basilides who – among other things, no doubt – was a fierce anti-Semite. Jung also adopted Gnostic terminology to articulate his message to "the dead", including the Gnostic/metaphysical distinction between *Pleroma* and *Creatura*.

To contextualize these remarks, in Sermon One, Jung informs us that Basilides' orations were delivered at the insistent demand of "the dead" (who are explicitly identified as Christians) because they had just returned from Jerusalem, where they "found not what they sought". The tacit implication of this remark could be that a Biblical faith, Jewish or Christian, could not address their questions, or fill the spiritual vacuum they were experiencing. In his second sermon, Jung/Basilides invokes Helios – the Sun – as the source of all Life, and another pagan entity or "hypostasis", Abraxas, known as the "God above God" – or more specifically, in this case, above Helios. The God of the Bible, known variously as Elohim, Jehovah or Adonai, addressed by the faithful as our Creator, Judge and Redeemer, is completely thrust aside, and never even mentioned here. Nor is Jesus.

Sermon Four contains an even more startling declaration. Addressing "the dead", Basilides says boldly:

> For me, to whom knowledge hath been given of the multiplicity and diversity of gods, it is well. But woe unto you, who replace these incompatible many with a single god. For in so doing, ye beget the torment which is bred from not understanding, and ye mutilate the creature whose nature and aim is distinctiveness. How can you be true to your own nature when you try to change the many into one? What you do unto the gods is likewise done unto you. Ye all become equal and thus is your nature maimed.
>
> (Jung and Jaffé, 1962, appendix 5, pp. 385–386)

A little bit further below, Jung/Basilides goes on to assert that: "Numberless gods await the human state. Numberless gods have been men. Man cometh from the gods and he goeth unto god" (MDR, appendix 5, p. 386).

Even if we make a generous allowance for Jung's state of mind at the time, it is difficult to imagine why the author of these lines would ever pose as a representative or defender of Christian civilization, and reproach the Jewish people – or indeed, anyone – with an anti-Christian bias. Clearly, this is a case of the pot calling the kettle black. Why? Because in the first stanza from Sermon Four, Jung, channeling Basilides, repudiates monotheism altogether, arguing that those who seek to "change the many into one" do so at the cost of inner torment and self-mutilation. In the second stanza quoted above, he flatly contradicts the Christian doctrine of the Incarnation, which stipulates that God became man once – and *only* once – in human history, and that this pivotal event was a prelude to the crucifixion, an event which Hegel called "the hinge of history"; the moment of redemption, which offers hope of forgiveness to all humankind. Instead, he says, "Numberless gods have become men ...", a statement which, if true, robs the Incarnation and crucifixion of Jesus of Nazareth of their pivotal role in the drama of Grace and Redemption, reducing them to the status of complete non-events.

Finally, another feature of Jung's *Seven Sermons* that merit careful scrutiny are the links Jung, following Nietzsche, makes between monotheism and the pursuit of human equality. The overarching message of the *Seven Sermons* is that each and every person should strive to realize and express their distinctiveness or individuality. But he seems to regard both Jewish and Christian piety as obstacles to this goal. For example, he wrote:

> How can you be true to your own nature when you try to change the many into one? What you do unto the gods is likewise done unto you. Ye all become equal and thus is your nature maimed.
>
> (Jung and Jaffé, 1962, appendix 5, pp. 385–386)

Evidently, then, Jung equated the idea of equality with a dreary uniformity that erases or effaces difference and distinctiveness; an idea that was commonplace among conservative and aristocratic critics of democratic social movements in the nineteenth and twentieth centuries. The idea that equality of rights and responsibilities, of opportunity and obligation, are perfectly compatible with a frank recognition – indeed, a robust celebration – of individual differences never occurred to him. Thus, in Jung's estimation, the ostensibly monotheist impulse to promote equality warps our psyches and disfigures our spiritual lives, rather than elevating our individual and collective spirits.

Jung's rejection of anything remotely resembling a monotheist conception of Deity is also evident in *The Red Book: Liber Novus*, a posthumously published work that he worked on from 1916 until 1930. The book consists of three sections: *Liber Primus* (First Book), *Liber Secundus* (Second Book) and a final section called *Scrutinies* that contains an Epilogue and several appendixes. The book is written in Gothic German script and is lavishly illustrated with original drawings and paintings by Jung, many of which are stunningly beautiful to behold. According to Jung and his followers, the book documents pivotal episodes in Jung's *nekiya*, or voyage to the underworld – his celebrated confrontation with the collective unconscious. A more detached and prosaic assessment might be that *The Red Book* chronicles Jung's prolonged and sometimes desperate attempts to manage and understand the mental and spiritual crises that engulfed him after his break with Freud, and his frequent fears of going – or indeed, of already being – mad. These urgent concerns are intimately interwoven with a long series of meditations on the relationship between madness and divine revelation, and the relationship between Judaism, Christianity and paganism, which are couched in the form of dialogues between the anonymous hero of the book and several imaginary interlocutors, including the Red One (whom Jung suspects is the Devil), an Egyptian anchorite (who is explicitly Christian), Elijah the Prophet, Salomé, a Herodian princess and a ghostly figure named Philemon, who is a "pagan who runs alongside our Christian religion" (p. 259).

Despite his deepening involvement with Philemon as the book unfolds, Jung is intent on establishing his allegiance to Christianity at the outset. But his efforts in this direction are already fraught with hints of heresy. For example, in *Liber Primus*, Jung's hero declares:

> Is there any one among you who believes he can be spared the way? Can he swindle his way past the pain of Christ? I say "Such a one deceives himself to his own detriment ... No one can be spared the pain of Christ, since his way leads to what is to come. You should all become Christs".
>
> (Jung, 2009, p. 234)

Unfortunately for Jung, Jesus said that he was "the way, the truth and the life" (John, 14:6), the "alpha and the omega" (Revelation, 1:8), not a second John the Baptist, a harbinger of the Aquarian Age, or a newer, emergent phase of human development (or consciousness) that will eventually overshadow or supersede his teaching. Moreover, if he was truly the Son of God, then the admonition "You should all become Christs" is an impossible demand, which rests on a fundamental misunderstanding (or deliberate misreading) of Christian doctrine. Nevertheless, in *Liber Secundus*, in his first encounter with the Red One, Jung's hero (or his authorial persona) declares again that

> no one is allowed to avoid the mysteries of the Christian religion unpunished. I repeat: he whose heart has not been broken over the Lord Jesus Christ drags a pagan around in himself, who holds him back from the best.
>
> (Jung, 2009, p. 260)

Evidently, the Red One, Jung's interlocutor at this juncture, accuses him of "sophistry", to which Jung replies:

> You're stubborn ... it is hardly a coincidence that the whole world has become Christian

Then the Red One objects that there are Jews who are good people, and have no need of Christian teaching, Jung replies with the following question:

> have you never noticed that the Jew himself lacks something – one in his head, another in his heart, and he himself feels that he lacks something?

The Red One then objects that Jung sounds like a "Jew hater". Jung responds as follows:

> you speak like all those Jews who accuse anyone of Jew hating who does not have a completely favorable judgment, while they themselves make the bloodiest jokes about their own kind. Since the Jews only too clearly feel that particular lack and yet do not want to admit it, they are extremely sensitive to criticism.
>
> (Jung, 2009, p. 260)

Obviously, Jung's remarks are intended to affirm his allegiance to Christianity, to assert that Jews are spiritually deficient or defective (in some vague and ill-defined way), and defend himself against the charge of anti-Semitism. These imaginary exchanges position Jung as a low-intensity/high-brow anti-Semite who believes that "the whole world has become Christian" and that Jews must lack "something" in their heads and hearts to remain Jewish.

Somewhat later in *The Red Book*, while wandering across a desert, Jung's hero comes across a man identified as the Anchorite, who devoted his entire life to the study of one book, the Bible. Jung expresses astonishment at the Anchorite's ability to discern inexhaustible depths of meaning in the text and says:

> If I understand you correctly, you think that the holy writings of the New Testament also have a doubleness, an exoteric and an esoteric meaning as a few Jewish scholars contend concerning their holy books.
>
> (Jung, 2009, p. 268)

To which the Anchorite responds: "This bad superstition is far from me", and proceeds to make a disparaging comparison between Philo Judaeus, whose notion of the Logos was "dead" and abstract, and the author of the Gospel of John, for whom the Logos is entirely alive and accessible to men. That being so, it is instructive to note that the Gospel of John is the most overtly anti-Semitic of all the gospels. It has Jesus addressing Jewish skeptics who doubt him as follows:

> You are of your father the devil, and your will is to do your father's desires. He was a murderer from the beginning, and has nothing to do with the truth, because there is no truth in him. When he lies, he speaks according to his own nature, for he is a liar and the father of lies.
>
> (John, 8: 44)

In a subsequent conversation with the Anchorite, Jung's hero says that Christian teaching really has little or nothing to do with the historical Jesus, but is simply a revised and refined version of the Egyptian myth of Osiris, who also suffered, died and was resurrected, to which the Anchorite replied: "If you say that our old teachings were less adequate expressions of Christianity, then I am more likely to agree with you" (Jung, 2009, p. 272). Taken together, the tacit implication of these remarks appears to be that Jews misinterpret their own sacred texts, which provide little more than verbal and conceptual props for the Christian religion to build on, while the cult of Osiris offered pagans a distorted and fragmentary premonition of the truth; one at least as important to contemporary Christians as the Jewish scriptures.

Not surprisingly, then, Jung's own foray into Biblical exegesis in *The Red Book* does not inspire confidence, despite the fact that his own father and maternal grandfather were accomplished Hebraists and Old Testament scholars. In one deeply disturbing passage, Jung invokes a passage in second Kings (4: 32–37), which describes a healing ritual performed by Elisha on the only son of the Shunammite. The Biblical passages read as follows:

> Elisha came into the house, and there was the boy, laid out dead on his couch. He went in, shut the door behind the two of them, and prayed to the Lord. Then he mounted the bed and placed himself over the child. He put his mouth on its mouth, his hands and its hands, as he bent over it. And the body of the child became warm. He stepped down, walked once up and down the room, then mounted and bent over him. Whereupon the boy sneezed seven times. And the boy opened his eyes.
>
> (II Kings, 4: 32–35)

In Jung's rendering of this passage in *The Red Book*, Elisha's life-saving intervention was actually a pedophilic and necrophilous violation of the deceased, rather than an attempt to infuse life back into his seemingly lifeless body. Here is the pertinent passage, with the Biblical allusion rendered in italics.

> What is this crazy desire craving satisfaction? Whose mad cries are these? ... Are you demanding a lusty comingling with corpses? I spoke of "acceptance" – but you to demand to "seize, embrace, copulate?" Are you demanding the desecration of the dead? *That prophet, you say, lay on the child, and placed his mouth over the child's mouth, and his eyes on its eyes, and his hands on its hands and thus he splays himself over the boy, so that the child's body becomes warm again. But he rose again and went here and there before he mounted anew and spread himself over him again. The boy snorted seven times. Then the boy opened his eyes.* So shall your acceptance be, so shall you accept, not cool, not superior, not thought out, not obsequious, not as a self-chastisement, but with pleasure, precisely with this ambiguous impure pleasure, whose ambiguity enables it to unite with the higher, with that holy-evil pleasure of which you do not know whether it be virtue or vice ... One wakens the dead with this pleasure.
>
> (Jung, 2009, p. 304)

Judging by this passage, when he wrote these words, Jung was probably wrestling with some deeply disturbing sexual fantasies of a necrophilous and pedophilic character, and struggling to integrate them into his psyche and self-image, somehow. But in order to do so, he first had to endow them with positive significance. Some may consider his efforts in this direction "transgressive" in Nietzsche's sense, and therefore evidence of courage or a superior wisdom that ventures "beyond good and evil". Others will object that Jung was simply flailing about without taking a principled stand, flirting with the idea that necrophilia and pedophilia are "acceptable" desires. Either way, his invocation of Elisha's healing ritual was a desperate and far-fetched gesture, intended to bestow a measure of vicarious "holiness" on an "impure" "evil pleasure" which could somehow "waken the dead". Whatever the author of Second Kings sought to convey, this was clearly not it. That being so, one wonders whether Jung's hermeneutic overreach was meant to mask or manage fears of being mad, by yoking the ideas of "holiness" and "pleasure" to fantasies of sheer depravity.

Several Jung scholars speculate that this weird and disquieting passage in *The Red Book* reflects the fact that Jung himself was sexually assaulted by an older man sometime in his childhood or his teenage years. There are very good grounds for supposing this is true. After all, in a letter to Freud, dated October 28, 1907, Jung attempted to explain his recent tardiness in responding to Freud's voluminous correspondence with a stunning confession. He said:

> Actually – and I confess this to you with a struggle – I have a boundless admiration for you both as a man and a researcher, and I bear you no conscious grudge. So the self-preservation complex does not come from there; it is rather that my veneration for you has something of the character of a "religious" crush. Though it does not really bother me, I still feel it is disgusting and ridiculous because of its undeniable erotic undertone. This abominable feelings comes from the fact that as a boy I was the victim of a sexual assault by a man I once worshipped ...
>
> This feeling, which I still have not quite got rid of, hampers me considerably. Another manifestation of it is that I find that psychological insight makes relations with colleagues who have a strong transference to me downright disgusting. I therefore fear your confidence. I also fear the same reaction from you when I speak of my intimate affairs. Consequently I skirt around such things as much as possible, for, to my feeling, at any rate, every intimate relationship turns out after a while to be sentimental and banal or exhibitionistic ...
>
> I think I owe you this explanation. I would rather not have said it.
> With kindest regards,
> Most sincerely yours, Jung
>
> (McGuire, 1974, p. 95)

Judging from this letter, then, the 32-year-old Jung was still struggling with after-effects of an early sexual trauma which adversely impacted his capacity for intimate relationships with men, complicating his professional life in various ways. Indeed, by his own admission, his feelings toward Freud were "disgusting", "ridiculous" and "abominable" to him, making Jung uncomfortable in Freud's presence. Jung's candor at this juncture took considerable courage, and in retrospect, one wonders what kind of response he expected, and in due course, received in light of this thundering revelation. One assumes that the response was disappointing, or at the very least, inadequate to resolve his lingering inner conflicts, because the after-effects of this trauma still reverberate through *The Red Book*, composed many years later. While Jung's age at the time of his trauma, and the identity of the man he was intimate with, have not been ascertained with certainty, the *quality* of that experience (from Jung's point of view) is captured in this passage from *The Red Book* in the chapter called "The Opening of the Egg" where he writes:

> While he rises, I go down. When I conquered the God, his force streamed into me. But when the God rested in the egg and awaited his beginning, my force went into him. And when he rose up radiantly, I lay on my face. He took my life with him. All my force was in him now. My soul swam like a fish in his sea of fire. But I lay in the frightful cool of the shadows of the earth and sank deeper and deeper into the lowest darkness. All light had left me. The God rose in the Eastern lands and I fell into the horror of the underworld. I lay there like a child bearer cruelly mauled and bleeding her life into the child, uniting life and death in a dying glance, the day's mother, the night's prey. My God had torn me apart terribly, he had drunk the juice of my life, he had drunk my highest power into him and become marvelous and strong like the sun ... He had taken my wings from me ... and the power of my will disappeared with him. He left me powerless and groaning.
>
> (Jung, 2009, p. 287)

Now, I leave it to others to discern the archetypal or esoteric meaning(s) this passage contains (or alludes to). But considered simply as a description of an unhappy sexual encounter – perhaps, indeed, Jung's first? – it sounds extremely intense, but also joyless and ultimately, devastating. "All light had left me." His God/lover had "torn me apart terribly", robbed him of his strength and his will. Indeed, Jung described this encounter as an interaction involving a net transfer of strength and "power" from himself to his "God", leaving him "powerless and groaning". Jung felt shattered and then abandoned, as he says in the following paragraph.

> Cruelly and unthinkably the sunbird spread its wings and flew up into infinite space. I was left with the broken shells and the miserable casing of his beginning, the emptiness of the depth opened up beneath me.
>
> (Jung, 2009, p. 287)

Leaving the specifically sexual dimension of this experience aside, for the moment, Jung's encounter with this older man rendered his "God" much stronger, more powerful, and Jung himself much weaker, at least in his own estimation. Though he talked about feelings that were ridiculous, abominable, and so on, in Freud's presence, Jung did not raise the issues of power and powerlessness in his correspondence. Nevertheless, if this passage from *The Red Book* is any indication, they were very salient at the time, and probably colored his fears and feelings toward Freud considerably, fueling a deep desire for revenge. This unrequited longing for revenge probably accounts for the famous "Siegfried dream" of December 18, 1913, in which Jung kills his "hero" – a condensation, one supposes, of Sigmund Freud and his abuser – and feels wracked with guilt afterwards (Kerr, 1993, p. 487). And this, in turn, partially accounts for the ferocity of his attacks on "Jewish psychology" and his efforts to enfeeble or eliminate the IPA, the organization Freud founded, during his period as *President of the General Medical Society for Psychotherapy*.

That said, it would be rash and needlessly reductionistic to assume that this youthful trauma was the only or even the main source of difficulty leading to Jung's rupture with Freud. There were so many! Jung's Christian upbringing and his sexual trauma were salient factors. But so was his visceral revulsion at Freud's positivism, rationalism and mechanistic materialism, which were quite deep and genuine in their own right. There is also the fact that Jung possessed a very creative, independent spirit, and that he chafed under the dogmatism attached to Freud's libido theory. Then again, rightly or wrongly, he suspected that Freud had a clandestine affair with his sister-in-law, Minna Bernays, and had good reason to do so. Indeed, Jung's eventual decision to live openly with his wife and his mistress, Antonia Wolff (1888–1953), may have been a conscious reaction against the (actual or perceived) hypocrisy of Freud, who (in Jung's view, anyway) tried to hide his extra-marital entanglements from public view (Burston, 1999).

In any case, there were many reasons why the friendship between Freud and Jung went awry, and it is quite likely that *all* of them colored his attitude toward Jews and Judaism for a time. But the fact remains that his breach with Freud impacted his attitude toward Jews negatively, and though he denied it, this was readily apparent to two of Jewish followers, James Kirsch and Erich Neumann, whose relationships with Jung we examine in the following chapter.

Note

1 Otto Weininger (1880–1903) was the Viennese author of a popular book entitled *Sex and Character*, which was published mere months before he took his own life. In it, he also suggested that women lack souls, and that Jews

resemble women (on several counts). His ideas were popular with the Nazis despite his Jewish ancestry, which Weinenger himself vigorously repudiated.

References

Burston, D. 1994. "Freud, the Serpent and the Sexual Enlightenment of Children." *The International Forum of Psychoanalysis* 3, pp. 205–219.

Burston, D. 1999. "Archetype and interpretation". *The Psychoanalytic Review* 86,no. 1, pp. 35–62.

Drob, S. 2010. *Kabbalistic Visions: C.G. Jung and Jewish Mysticism.* New Orleans: Spring Journal Books.

Elon, A. 2002. *The Pity of It All: A History of the Jews in Germany 1743-1933.* New York: Picador.

Freud, S. 1909. *Analysis of a Phobia in a Five Year Old Boy.* London: Hogarth Press, *Standard Edition*, 1957, 10, pp. 1–145, 1955.

Freud, S. 1913. *Totem and Taboo.* London: Hogarth Press, Standard Edition, 1957, 13, pp. 1–161.

Freud, S. 1914. *On the History of the Psychoanalytic Movement.* London: Hogarth Press, *Standard Edition*, 1957, vol. 14, pp. 6–66.

Freud, S. 1939. *Moses and Monotheism.* London: Hogarth Press, *Standard Edition*, 23, pp. 1–137.

Harms, E. 1946 "Carl Gustav Jung: Defender of Freud and the Jews", reprinted in Maidenbaum, A. and Martin, S. *Lingering Shadows: Freudians, Jungians and Anti-Semitism.* New York: Shamabala, 1991.

Hitler, A. 1925. *Mein Kampf.* Trans, Ralph Mannheim. New York: Houghton Miflin.

Jung, C.G., 2009. *The Red Book: Liber Novus.* Edited by Sonu Shanmdasani, New York: W.W.Norton.

Jung, C.G. and Jaffé, A. 1962. *Memories, Dreams, Reflections.* New York: Vintage.

Kerr, J. 1993. *A Most Dangerous Method: The Story of Jung, Freud and Sabina Spielrein.* New York: Knopf.

Lammers, A.C. 2011. *The Jung-Kirsch Letters: The Correspondence of C.G. Jung and James Kirsch.* New York: Routledge.

McGuire, W., ed. 1974. *The Freud-Jung Letters.* Princeton, NJ: Princeton University Press.

Neumann, M. 2015. *The Relationship Between C.G. Jung and Erich Neumann Based on Their Correspondence.* Ashville, NC: Chiron Publications.

Schorske, C. 1981. *Fin-de-Siécle Vienna: Politics and Culture.* New York: Vintage Books.

Sherry, J. 1991. "The Case of Jung's Alleged Anti-Semitism", in *Lingering Shadows: Jungians, Freudians and Anti-Semitism*, Maidenbaum, A. and Martin, S., eds, London: Shamabala, pp. 117–132.

Sherry, J. 2010. *C.G. Jung: Avant-Garde Conservative*. Palgrave MacMillen. Cham: Switzerland.

Stein, R. 1989. "Jung's 'Mana' Personality in the Nazi Era", in *Lingering Shadows: Jungians, Freudians and Anti-Semitism*, Maidenbaum A. and Martin, S. eds, London: Shambala.

Stern, K. 1951. *The Pillar of Fire*. New York: Image Books.

Tanach: A New Translation of The Holy Scriptures, 1985, Philadelphia, PA: Jewish Publication Society.

4 Judaism, Zionism and analytical psychology
1933–1959

While we may engage in a solitary search for self-knowledge, and should always endeavor to do so, at the end of the day, we discover and reveal ourselves most in dialogue and relationships with others. That being so, there are valuable lessons to be learned from Jung's dealings with two of his Jewish followers, notably, James Kirsch and Erich Neumann, and with his erstwhile friend and pupil, Hans Trüb, who was not Jewish, but whose later work was profoundly influenced by the Jewish philosopher Martin Buber.

James Kirsch

Let's begin with James Kirsch (1901–1989). Kirsch was one of five children born in Guatemala City to a German-Jewish businessman and his wife. Once his father's business was established, James and his siblings returned to Berlin with their mother in 1907 in order to acquire a proper education. Kirsch was a gifted student who studied medicine at the University of Heidelberg, where he joined the Zionist Blau-Weiss (Blue and White) Society, where he befriended Erich Fromm and Ernst Simon, who remained his lifelong friends. On completing his medical studies, he returned to Berlin for a residency in psychiatry and commenced an unsatisfactory Freudian analysis that lasted two years. Having read Jung's book *Psychological Types*, he then wrote to Jung in 1928 and arranged to do an analysis with Jung in 1929. His analysis with Jung lasted 60 hours but was augmented in the following months and years with analytic sessions with Toni Wolff, Liliane Frey and C.A. ("Freddy") Meier.

In 1933, Hitler seized power in Germany. Kirsch feared for his life, and together with his first wife and their children, fled to Tel Aviv, where he quickly became disenchanted with Zionism. Longing for a more comfortable life, he moved to London with his second wife in 1935, and in 1940, in the midst of the blitzkrieg, moved to the United States, eventually settling in Los Angeles. Along with Max Zeller and several other German-Jewish analysts, Kirsch founded the Jungian community in Los Angeles, and remained an active member until 1988, one year before his death.

Kirsch's correspondence with Jung spans the years 1929–1961 and is full of interesting ideas and anecdotes. Ann Conrad Lammers, who edited the Jung–Kirsch letters, notes that Jung benefited from Kirsch's decision, while in Israel, to study Hebrew, and to read biblical texts and commentaries in the original language. This somewhat belated immersion in his religious heritage provided Kirsch with material for many of his subsequent publications. Lammers also notes that Jung benefited from Kirsch's friendship and support while he gradually "came to terms with the fact that, in certain writings of the 1930s, he had borrowed words and phrases from the lexicon of anti-Semitism". Lammers comments:

> Whether or not he intended it, some of Jung's writings at the time had the potential to do harm, a fact which he came to recognize, and – privately, at least – to confess. Jung always denied having anti-Semitic intentions, and Kirsch also denied it on his behalf.
>
> (Lammers, 2011, p. xxxii)

Lammers then points out that public reaction to these publications was strong and immediate, and that Kirsch himself was baffled and dismayed by Jung's utterances in 1933–1934. By way of reply, notes Lammers, Jung's correspondence with Kirsch:

> makes it clear that he (Jung) is desperately serious about straightening out the record and that he urgently wants Kirsch on his side in the battle that has erupted. Kirsch accepts Jung's account and organizes public support for him. From then on he sends Jung every kind of educational help he can. Starting in the early 1930's, Jung relies on Kirsch as a tutor, then as a loyal critic, and finally as a staunch defender.
>
> (Lammers, 2011, p. xxxiii)

Lammers' description of the relationship between Jung and Kirsch is instructive, as far as it goes. But she says that Jung merely borrowed "words and phrases" from the anti-Semitic lexicon, as if one can do that innocently in a time of great peril. Furthermore, she tiptoed around the fact that Jung did not apologize *publicly* for his harmful utterances.

From her point of view, perhaps, a private apology, or series of apologies – to close friends, confidantes and followers of Jewish heritage – coupled with a steadfast denial of anti-Semitic attitudes in public, was an adequate, or perhaps, even an admirable response. She never raises the possibility that Kirsch may have idealized Jung so intensely that his attitude was *overprotective*, shielding Jung from well-deserved criticism, and an opportunity for deeper and more honest soul-searching on this score.

Besides, there are some subtle, complicated and telling features to their lengthy correspondence that cannot be captured in a summary this brief. For example, on May 7, 1934, Kirsch wrote to Jung that he was dumbfounded by his recent statement that Jews are incapable of creating their own culture because, said Jung, "... all of his (the Jew's) instincts and talents presuppose a more or less civilized host-people for their development". According to Kirsch, however, what Jung wrote is only true of Jews living in the diaspora, or what Zionists of that era termed "Galut Jews". In Palestine, wrote Kirsch, Jews are living "as a people, resident, earthbound and self-reliant, not in the middle of another culture", adding: "I wish you could see some of these new types of Jews".

Having praised the "earthbound and self-reliant" new Zionist man, Kirsch nevertheless makes an astonishing concession. He writes:

> In Faulhaber's words, since Christ, the Jews have been excluded from the revelation. We made a vital mistake by rejecting Christ. Christ *is* the repressed complex of the Jew. However, just as everything changes in the individual life of a person as soon as a repressed complex enters into consciousness and comes alive, in the same way, things can change collectively – and also creatively – with our repressed Christ complex.
>
> (Kirsch, in Lammers, 2011, p. 43)

Then Kirsch concludes:

> We are dealing with a collective standstill, a repression with all its consequences. Also, we are not nomads, but a restless people that has lost its living God, despite all the warnings of the prophets. We even pronounced the dreadful word about Christ: His blood be upon our head and that of our children.
>
> (Kirsch, in Lammers, 2011, p. 43)

It is hard to overstate the oddity of these statements. On the one hand, Kirsch pushes back against Jung and affirms the vitality and uniqueness of Jewish culture. (He does this repeatedly in the course of their early correspondence.) On the other hand, he concedes to Faulhaber that the Jews' rejection of Jesus as the Messiah means that they have been "excluded from the revelation", i.e. are spiritually deficient or stillborn, in some sense. Then he adds that Jews are not nomads, as Jung maintained, but restless, having lost their "living God", even claiming that Jews pronounced the fateful words: "His blood be upon our head and that of our children" (Matthew 27:25).

Now, in the interests of clarity, permit me to point out that it is one thing to have rejected the proposition that Jesus is the Messiah, and quite another to claim (collective) responsibility for his death. The former is undoubtedly true, while the latter is patently false. Nevertheless, Kirsch proposed that Jews are guilty on both counts – a rhetorical move that appeals deeply and directly to the anti-Semitic imagination, and which Jung himself probably shared. In fact, however, there is no evidence (outside of the Gospel of Matthew) that the Jews present at the trial of Jesus claimed collective responsibility for his crucifixion, or that if they did, that their attitudes were in any way representative of the general population's feelings toward Jesus at the time. Indeed, the preponderance of evidence *strongly* suggests that this was actually not the case, and that these words were attributed to the mob to stoke anti-Semitic feelings among Greek-speaking Christians (Crossan, 1996; Ruether, 1997). Moreover, history demonstrates that the blood curse, as it is called, was remarkably successful in inciting violence and murder against hundreds of thousands, if not millions of Jews over the centuries (Carroll, 2002). To suggest that the Jews *knowingly* and *collectively* called this dreadful curse upon themselves is utterly bizarre, from a Jewish perspective. Seen in this light, Kirsch's concession to Faulhaber makes his recently renewed commitment to his Jewish heritage seem hollow or equivocal at best; a curious posture which, in some carefully concealed way, was profoundly disfigured by internalized anti-Semitism, of which he himself was unconscious.

That being so, it is instructive to note that in his reply to Kirsch, dated May 26, 1934, Jung acknowledged his complete *agreement* with Kirsch's assessment of the "Christ-complex" that Jews allegedly struggled with (unconsciously, for the most part) for two millennia, and then, toward the end of the letter, scolded him gently for imagining, even briefly, that he could really be an anti-Semite. Jung then defended his assertion that Jews are incapable of creating their own culture, but gave it a new and more positive twist than he had previously, suggesting now that as the bearers of their host culture, the task Jews presumably take on is actually extremely demanding; a task for which they are well suited, but which is unlikely to leave much energy or time for developing a culture of their own. This way of framing the issue suggests that the relationship of Jews to their host culture is not parasitic, but symbiotic, i.e. of benefit to both parties. He also hastened to point out that he did not entirely rule out the possibility that the return of Jews to Palestine might engender something new and meaningful, adding, however, that he is not yet convinced that it will and that only time would tell.

On June 8, Kirsch replied that he was greatly relieved by Jung's most recent letter. To apologize for thinking, however briefly, that his beloved teacher was somewhat anti-Semitic, he observed that his image of Jung was "somewhat darkened" by a remark of his former analyst, Toni Wolff, who evidently told Kirsch that if Jung were a German, he would have voted for the Nazis (in 1933). Given how intimate Wolff's relationship with Jung was, both personally and professionally, one wonders why she said something this damning if it did not contain a kernel of truth, and why Jung subsequently passed over this matter in silence. In any case, Kirsch cheerfully maintained, while he wondered and worried at this statement of Wolff's, he had never *really* imagined that Jung is an anti-Semite.

In the remainder of this long letter, Kirsch gave Jung a useful thumbnail sketch of Jewish history and culture in the West and used it to sharpen his initial critique of Jung's statement that Jews lack a culture of their own. Kirsch cited the survival of the Hebrew language, and the creative energy embodied in Jewish philosophy and literature, as evidence of a uniquely Jewish culture, and now argued, contra Jung, that Jews only lacked a culture of their own in the wake of the Jewish Enlightenment, or Haskalah, when Jews assimilated to European culture in large numbers. Indeed, he mentions Heine in this regard and attributed the emergence of such "inspiring but destructive" figures as Marx and Freud – both ardent admirers of Heine's – to the fact that in this historical period, Jews "repressed" their Jewishness in favor of a "soulless materialism", and commended Jung for discovering the creative depths of the "Germanic soul" (sic), which protests mightily against their ideas.

However, Kirsch still maintained that Jewish culture, even at its most creative and dynamic, is hobbled by the "Christ complex". For example, he wrote that Chassidism was short lived "because it failed to find the historic thread from the prophets to Jesus", adding that: "For me, at least, it is only through you that it became possible to understand the experience of the prophets, the Messianic idea, and to rediscover what was lost to the consciousness of the Jewish people." Kirsch concluded this strange letter with an exuberant endorsement of the Zionist movement, saying that he is strongly and "unconditionally bound to this new experiment".

In truth, however, one year later, Kirsch and his (second) wife left Palestine for London. Indeed, he wrote to Jung from London on June 19, 1935, saying that the reason for his departure was not the land of Palestine, but – the Jews! He complained that the Jews "do not accept the land and the primitiveness there" and as a result, attempt (consciously and unconsciously) to perpetuate their exile – an assertion that sounds suspiciously like a projection or rationalization for his own *abandonment* of the Zionist project. Evidently, Kirsch found the Zionists in Tel Aviv too anti-religious for his taste and accused them of focusing relentlessly on economic development for the benefit of future generations, sacrificing *individuation* in the process. In short, it appears, they were largely unresponsive to Kirsch's ambassadorial overtures on Jung's behalf, which were probably rendered doubly ineffective by the disintegration of his first marriage.[1] In any case, Kirsch's departure left him with few friends in Palestine. Fortunately for Jung, he had another devoted friend and follower in Tel Aviv, Erich Neumann.

Erich Neumann

Erich Neumann (1905–1960) was born in Berlin. From an early age, Neumann was deeply interested in philosophy, psychology, art, poetry and the roots of Jewish identity. He earned a doctorate in philosophy from the University of Erlangen on the mystical language philosophy of Johann Arnold Kanne (1773–1824) in 1927, and became interested in psychotherapy, and commenced his medical training at the prestigious Friederich-Wilhelms University in Berlin. He completed his studies in 1933, but could not practice because of the Nazis' racial laws. After an exchange of letters, he met with Jung in Zürich in October 1933 and worked with him there for several months. Neumann's wife, Julie and one-year-old son, Micha, emigrated to Tel Aviv in February 1934, while Erich lingered on in Europe until May. At some undetermined point just before his departure for Palestine, Neumann received a copy of "On the Present Situation of Psychotherapy" from Toni Wolff and wrote to Jung immediately to express his disappointment and dismay. This long and remarkable letter begins on a plaintive note, but becomes more angry and incredulous as Neumann proceeds. Neumann warned Jung that he was inviting misinterpretation, that his words would be experienced and interpreted in ways that were at odds with his original intentions; that the Germanic unconscious, so called, is as riddled with "filth" and "rottenness" as its Jewish/Freudian counterpart; that Jung celebrated the bloodthirsty irrationalism of the Nazi movement, rather than standing in principled opposition to it; that Jung's knowledge of Jews and Judaism was fragmentary, and gleaned from remote and unreliable sources; that Jung's remarks about the Jewish psyche were overly shaped by his experience with Freud; that movements like Hasidism and Zionism attest to the creative dynamism still dormant in the Jewish soul, which Neumann vastly preferred to the "rigid" "brutal" "stolid" and "submissive" character of National Socialist rites and rallies.

Evidently, Jung and Neumann met once more before his departure for Tel Aviv and agreed to address their differences on this score in their correspondence; a correspondence interrupted by WWII which spans the years 1933–1940 and 1945–1959. As was the case with Kirsch, the relationships between Judaism and Christianity, between Jews and Germans, the Zionist movement, Hasidism and so on were frequent topics of discussion, especially before the war. And as was the case with Kirsch, the overall tone of this correspondence is mostly cordial and respectful, even quite affectionate in spots. Also, as with Kirsch, the two men agree that Judaism began as an extremely introverted religion, and that the advent of the Enlightenment shattered the remarkable cohesion of Jewish communities that existed prior to that point – although Neumann's application of Jung's theory of types to these materials and motifs is more complex and far reaching, at least in their correspondence, than Kirsch's was.

Nevertheless, in an addendum to another undated letter, composed later that same year, Neumann continued to prod – albeit more gently, now – at Jung's religious preconceptions in ways that Kirsch obviously did not, noting that they were also widely shared among his followers. For example, he wrote that:

> one must free oneself from Christian prejudices, which in a ridiculous way, see the Old Testament as a precursor of the New. It seems to me sometimes that even you have not fully freed yourself from the belief in progress on this point; from primitive tribe to developed Christendom, as the Church teaches. This is simply laziness. E.g. the children's nightmare of Y.H.W.H. as a God of vengeance and many other remnants of protestant theology and biblical criticism that still haunt the club.
>
> (Neumann in Liebscher, 2015, p. 70)

Then, somewhat further below, Neumann adds:

> the entire world's barbaric and disgusting anti-Judaism goes hand in hand with a wave of autarchic-nationalistic national individualism

and one that apparently faces an official explanation in which the unity of the human race is nailed as a Jewish lie amid the heathen national cults. Jewish-Christian chiliasm that strives for the thousand year kingdom of developed consciousness, i.e. not only an individual but a collective consciousness that changes the face of the earth, is threatened by an onslaught of heathen, settled and soil-bound archetypes, accommodated to the world, and being partly swallowed up by them.

This last comment was probably Neumann's indirect way of expressing his distaste for Jung's cordial relationship with Jakob Wilhelm Hauer, and other racist theorists who maintained that "the unity of the human race is ... a Jewish lie".

Alert to Neumann's continuing distress, Jung responded on April 27, 1935. He began by saying that most of Neumann's recent criticisms are correct, but that his own perspective is not so much prejudiced as "one-sided", and inevitably so, because all judgments reflect a particular point of view, and must be "one sided at first in order to be moderated later ...". However, he becomes more defensive as the letter unfolds, defending his decision to become President of the General Medical Society for Psychotherapy and his views on National Socialism. He then adds: "I think you do me an injustice when you assume that I regard the New Testament per se as a development of the Old Testament" (Liebscher, 2015, p. 104). On the face of it, Jung's arguments on this score sound perfectly sincere, though on reflection, and in fairness to Neumann, Jung did *not* contest Kirsch's (more or less) contemporaneous presentation of the relationship between the two faiths in precisely this light! However, further below, Jung goes on to say:

The Jew can best be understood as a sourdough whose effect must not go too far. If the nations of the earth were to be so cut off from their history and their link with the soil by Jewish fermentation as has happened to the German, then a reaction sets in, and then the entire nation does what every single individual should have done.

(Jung in Liebscher, 2015, p. 107)

Jung was speaking analogically, of course, something all of us do from time to time. But concerning the metaphor of fermentation, one wonders what Jung actually meant when he said that this process had gone "too far"? How far is too far, and why? And with those questions in mind, one also wonders what he imagines that "every single individual" in Germany should have done in order to avert the horrors that ensued shortly afterwards? Jung's reply is alarmingly short on specifics, leaving the answers to these questions completely open to conjecture.

Meanwhile, as if in concert with Jung's assessment that Jewish "fermentation" had gone too far, the Nazis had recently purged Germany's universities of all their Jewish faculty, a fact Jung did not address. Seen from Neumann's perspective, Jung's silence on this score probably felt remarkably tone-deaf. And that was merely the beginning, of course. On September 15, 1935, the Nazis introduced the Nuremberg Laws, which criminalized marriage (or indeed sexual intercourse of any kind) between Aryans and Jews, forbade German women under 45 from working in Jewish households, and deprived Jews of *all* rights of citizenship. In November of that year, these prohibitions were extended to Roma and to Blacks as well.

Six weeks after this heinous legislation was passed, on October 30, 1935, Jung gave a seminar in which he held forth on the subject of race mixing, albeit without directly referencing the Nuremberg Laws. In *C. G. Jung: Avant-Garde Conservative*, Jay Sherry quotes Jung saying that "race mixing" is something:

> against which our instincts always set up a resistance. Sometimes one thinks it is snobbish prejudice, but it is an instinctive prejudice, and the fact is that if distant races are mixed, the fertility is very low, as one sees with the white and the negro; a negro woman very rarely conceives from a white man. If she does, a mulatto is the result and he is apt to be a bad character. The Malays are a very distant race, very remote from the white man, and the mixture of Malay and white is as a rule bad.
>
> (Jung in Sherry, 2010, p. 152)

Sherry goes on to point out that during the seminar, Jung told Jolande Jacobi, a Jewish woman who converted to Catholicism during the course of her analysis with Jung: "You know, I would never like to have children from a person who has Jewish blood." Here an analyst was telling his former patient that he would never want to have children with her because of her "race". What to make of a remark like this?

I cannot imagine Jung being this candid with Neumann, even privately, which demonstrates that if he was being honest with Jacobi, Jung was *not* being honest with Neumann, or indeed, with himself, when he disclaimed any anti-Semitic prejudice. We can imagine how Neumann might have responded to a comment like this from the fact that one day earlier, on October 29, 1935, he wrote to Jung, complaining that analytical psychology is so deeply rooted in Christian–European culture that without realizing it, assimilated Jews (notably Heinz Westmann and James Kirsch) actually capitulate to a Christian perspective on their own ancestral faith, while presenting themselves as its most enlightened or authentic representatives. In Neumann's words:

> The understandable (to me) anti-Jewish thrust of the entire West, from Marcion to Harnack, from theology to psychology, has the effect on instinctless Jews – and many Jews are instinctless, as you know – of a Jewish self-poisoning process that was always charac-teristic of the tendency of Jews to avoid the bitter path of individu-ation through the path of being a pariah.
>
> (Neumann in Liebscher, 2015, p. 115)

These words convey the unmistakable impression that Neumann was determined not to erase or abandon his cultural heritage, even if meant remaining an outlier in Jung's world.

The correspondence between Jung and Neumann in 1933 and 1934 was somewhat erratic, for a variety of reasons, but the letters they exchanged were often lengthy and infused with passionate and care-fully wrought arguments and ideas. By contrast, the volume of letters exchanged in 1936 was quite meager, and the letters themselves not par-ticularly revealing. One reason for this is that after two years in Palestine Neumann was suffering from exhaustion, and expressed a need to with-draw temporarily from further work on "the Jewish question" and the Zionist movement. Another, no doubt, was that Neumann and his wife actually saw and spoke to Jung and Toni Wolff in person during a brief visit to Zürich that year – the last time they would visit Europe until 1947.

Meanwhile, and perhaps in response to the Nuremberg Laws passed the previous year, there was now talk about "too many Jews" altering the Swiss character of the Zürich Analytical Psychology Club, which first surfaced at the Club's annual meeting of 1936. Neumann was prob-ably unaware of this at the time. On this occasion, evidently, Jung was moved to say:

> that Jews are an important cultural factor in Europe, even though their racial difference cannot be denied. If they produce a bad effect, then the person who is being affected must seek for reasons within himself or herself. The Club should expose itself to such effects and consciously deal with them, instead of holding others responsible for an unpleasant influence.
>
> (Kirsch, 2000, p. 35)

Jung's feelings on the matter – that Jews are racially "different", but that this provided an opportunity for internal reflection, not grounds for exclusion – seemed to carry the day for a time. Nevertheless, discussions like these continued behind the scenes, resurfacing in 1940 as the war dragged on. And as a result, in 1944, Toni Wolff and Freddy Meier actually imposed a 10% quota on Jewish membership that lasted till 1950. The memo in which the quota was codified was circulated only among executive members, and effectively kept secret until a good friend of Neumann's – Jung's dentist, Siegmund Hurwitz (1904–1994), a Kabbalah scholar – refused to join the club until the quota was expunged from the Club's charter (Bair, 2003; Liebscher, 2015, p. xlix; p. 277).

That said, it is important to note that in 1936, the year Jung published "Wotan", conditions of life had become increasingly difficult for Jews in Germany. As Marion Kaplan notes in *Between Dignity and Despair: Jewish Life in Nazi Germany*, the steady degradation, immiseration and disintegration of Jewish communities and institutions that began in 1933, and intensified in 1935, was proceeding apace, and would soon reach a sickening crescendo on November 10, 1938 – Kristallnacht (Kaplan, 1998). Meanwhile, in 1937, Neumann's father, Eduard, perished from injuries sustained at the hands of German thugs – possibly the Gestapo a deep and irrevocable loss.

Though it is seldom (and only fleetingly) referenced in their correspondence at the time, living conditions for Jews in Palestine became increasingly difficult in 1936–1937 as well. In 1936, as the situation in Europe became more dire, the British halted all further Jewish immigration to Palestine and shelved their plans for creating a Jewish state, which they had announced almost two decades previously in the Balfour Declaration of 1917. They halted all further Jewish immigration in deference to the wishes of the Palestinian populace, and in particular, of their leader, Hajj Amin al-Husseini, the Grand Mufti of Jerusalem, who orchestrated bloody riots against the British and the Jews of Palestine in 1936 (Morris, 2001). Obviously, Neumann's life was impacted by these developments in ways that Kirsch's was not. In a letter dated December 5, 1938, Neumann referenced the nationwide pogrom called Kristallnacht that occurred in Germany and Austria one month earlier, saying worse was yet to come. Moreover, he said, he was acutely aware that he did not – and could not – know if he and his family would be among the survivors or not, lamenting the constant reminders of the precarious position of Jews in Palestine, and "reports that crowd in on one on a daily and hourly basis".

The year 1938 was a significant one for Neumann. His daughter Rahli was born, and his mother Zelma, who was supposed to join Neumann and his family in Tel Aviv, was stranded in London with her other son, Franz, only to resume her journey to Palestine after the war, in 1947. By 1939, Neumann began to tire of his relentless focus on the psychology of Jews and Judaism. On November 15, 1939, he wrote to Jung, saying:

> I am so tired of the Jews and the Jewish – and every free minute and every free thought belongs to these subjects, and I must protect myself from being swallowed up by this work.
>
> (Liebscher, 2015, p. 149)

Despite these misgivings, brought on by overwork, Neumann remained in Palestine to foster the growth of analytical psychology in what would eventually become the State of Israel. And despite (realistic) fears of Nazi armies invading Palestine, the years 1940–1945 were productive ones for Neumann. Having finally finished a book on Hasidism, he turned his attention away from Judaism and Zionism to focus primarily on developmental psychology and ethics. However, from December 7, 1940 to October 1, 1945, there was no further exchange of letters between Neumann and Jung, because no postal service was available between Switzerland and Israel. (Kirsch, by contrast, maintained intermittent contact during this interval, despite wartime conditions.)

All through 1934, Neumann had pressured Jung to take an interest in Hasidism and Kabbalah, but to no avail. But curiously, in 1944 Jung started to develop a deep interest in Kabbalah, and his philo-Semitic side came increasingly to the fore after his second heart attack in 1946, just as Neumann and he began to be in regular contact again. In the ensuing years, Jung developed warm friendships with Siegmund Hurwitz and with Gershom Scholem, another scholar of Kabbalism who, like Neumann himself, became a regular participant in the annual Eranos conferences in Ascona. From this point onwards, Kabbalistic symbols and motifs played an increasingly important part in the development of Jung's ideas (Drob, 2010).

In the years following WWII, Kirsch and Neumann maintained very different attitudes toward Jung. As a founding member of the Los Angeles Jungian community, Kirsch remained attached to "classical" Jungian ideas and approaches and reported frequently to Jung about his group's evolving controversies with their counterparts in San Francisco, who had a more "clinical" orientation. Kirsch was not only extremely loyal in this respect, but remained dependent on Jung and Toni Wolff to help him address his frequent and embarrassing extramarital entanglements with patients, which were attributed to his "inferior and insecure" anima. For the remainder of his life, however, he was held in high esteem in Zürich and maintained the same idealizing attitude he had adopted toward Jung prior to WWII.

Neumann was an altogether different story. Having developed his own depth psychological perspective during WWII – evidenced, among other things, in his modified theory of introversion and his notion of "centroversion" – he made many members of the Jung establishment – including Jung himself, at times – uncomfortable. One bone of contention was the Zürich Club's open disapproval of Neumann's book *Depth Psychology and A New Ethic*, which was written during WWII. Jung liked the book and eventually wrote an introduction to it. But many of Jung's followers, especially Toni Wolff and Jolande Jacobi, did not, and some of Jung's students even sought to expunge Neumann's (rather tame) references to the horrors of the Holocaust, possibly for fear of alienating their German colleagues, who were then subject to the Allied powers' program of "de-Nazification". As the conflicts between Neumann, Toni Wolff, C.A. Meier, Jolande Jacobi and several other members of Jung's inner circle heated up in the late 1940s and early 1950s, Jung adopted an increasingly passive, ambiguous and non-committal attitude toward these internal rows, as one might expect from a man of his years in awkward circumstances like these. This angered Neumann, who expressed his disappointment quite forcefully in two remarkably frank letters to Jung dated April 6 and April 9, 1949. And in a letter to Olga Fröbe-Kapteyn in 1949 on March 14 of that year, he said:

> Jung's behavior towards me is extremely moving and he cares in a way that truly affects me. Of course this has to be of higher importance to me than his weakness in individual cases, where, in my opinion, he is factually wrong at times. Nevertheless, the whole affair ... demonstrates to me the emergence of a reactionary Europe, which takes possession of Jung. Catholicism, individualism – well, those are words, but they are also powers, and everything rhymes in such a sad and fitting way with fascism and national socialism. Because of Jung's carelessness it has already been tremendously difficult so far to separate Jung and his work from the embarrassing, even catastrophic closeness to it.
>
> (Liebscher, 2015, pp. xlix–l)

This last sentence is particularly revealing, since it reveals the great embarrassment and difficulty Neumann experienced trying to defend Jung's good name against the onslaught of hostile critics both before and after WWII. To his credit, Jung finally rose to Neumann's defense on October 5, 1950, at a meeting convened in his home at Küsnacht, when he chastised Neumann's adversaries at length for being unreasonable and uncharitable. When or how the news of this event reached Neumann is unknown, but it must have gone a considerable distance toward mending their relationship, because the remainder of their correspondence, until Neumann's death in 1960, is unmarred by any hint of anger or disappointment.

Hans Trüb

One finds a partial parallel to Neumann's experience with Jung and his circle in the life and work of Hans Trüb (1889–1949), one of Jung's earliest and most trusted followers. Trüb was Toni Wolff's brother-in-law and analyzed Jung's wife, Emma. Trüb was not Jewish, but was quite religious, and from 1923 until his death in 1951, was in a close intellectual and spiritual rapport with the Jewish philosopher Martin Buber (1872–1965), who lectured at the Eranos conference in 1924. In *Jung: A Biography*, Deirdre Bair paints a very sympathetic portrait of Trüb's warm friendship with Emma Jung, and his dogged but ultimately unsuccessful efforts to reconcile his fondness for (and friendship with) Jung and his family with non-Jungian ideas and practices he gleaned from his evolving friendships with Buber, Ludwig Binswanger and several Christian theologians who, like Buber, espoused a kind of religious-socialist-communitarian philosophy that emphasized the need for social justice and active participation in communal life. Though he began as a trusted "insider" in Jung's circle, he ended up an outsider who was barely tolerated. Indeed, Trüb's brief Presidency of the Analytical Psychology Club (1919–1923) ended in disaster because it was animated by his desire to bring Jungian psychology into dialogue with other intellectual currents of the day, something which Jung and his followers had no wish to pursue. According to Deidre Bair, Jung detested Buber, who first called attention to the anti-Jewish (and less obviously, anti-Christian) implications of the *Seven Sermons to the Dead*, which Trüb had shared with him (Buber, 1952). And unlike Neumann, who managed to maintain a friendship with Jung despite serious disagreements with his followers, Trüb's determination to follow his own path forced him – after many failed efforts at reconciliation – to forfeit his friendships with Jung and his wife as well. Trüb's wife Susi, one of the original Club members, remained a (somewhat distant) member of the Club for many years afterwards, and only quit when her sister, Toni Wolff, vigorously discouraged her from pursuing the posthumous publication of Trüb's last book, *Healing Through Meeting*, which was subtitled "A Dialogue with the Psychology of C.G. Jung". Indeed, in a long letter to her sister, detailing her objections to Trüb's book, Toni Wolff revealed what Bair called "... an inability to understand the Jewish perspective, and what many others considered her innate anti-Semitism" (Bair, 2003). Indeed, Wolff wrote that her sister's late husband's relationships to Jewish philosophers, especially Buber, prevented him from discerning the real truth, namely, that the ultimate physician is none other than "... Jesus himself, who is wounded and killed as a healer and then becomes the divine doctor and savior". From that point onwards, Toni Wolff and Susi Wolff-Trüb were irrevocably estranged (Bair, 2003, pp. 540–543).

Note

1 Neumann's letter to Jung dated February 9, 1935, paints an alarming picture of Kirsch's state of mind during the breakup of his first marriage. See Liebscher (2015, pp. 84–88).

References

Bair, D. 2003. *Jung: A Biography.* New York: Little, Brown and Company.

Buber, M. 1952. *Eclipse of God: Studies in the Relation Between Philosophy and Religion,* reprinted by Humanities Press International, Atlantic Highlands: NJ, 1988.

Carroll, J. 2002. *Constantine's Sword: The Church and the Jews – A History.* Boston, MA: Houghton Miflin.

Crossan, J.D. 1996. *Who Killed Jesus: Exposing the Roots of Anti-Semitism in the Gospecl Story of the Death of Jesus.* San Francisco, CA: Harper and Row.

Drob, S. 2010. *Kabbalistic Vision: C. G. Jung and Jewish Mysticism.* New Orleans, LA: Spring Journal Books.

Kaplan, M. 1998. *Between Dignity and Despair: Jewish Life in Nazi Germany.* New York: Oxford University Press.

Kirsch, T. 2000. *The Jungians: A Comparative and Historical Perspective.* London: Routledge.

Lammers, A.C. ed., 2011. *The Jung-Kirsch Letters: The Correspondence of C.G. Jung and James Kirsch.* London: Routledge.

Liebscher, M. ed., 2015. *Analytical Psychology in Exile: The Correspondence of C. G. Jung and Erich Neumann.* Princeton, NJ: Princeton University Press.

Morris, B. 2001. *Righteous Victims: A History of the Zionist Arab Conflict.* New York: Random House.

Ruether, R. 1997. *Faith and Fratricide: The Theological Roots of Anti-Semitism.* Eugene, OR: WIPF & Stock Publishers.

Sherry, J. 2010. *C.G. Jung: Avant-Garde Conservative.* Cham, Switzerland: Palgrave MacMillan.

5 Rethinking the past

Vatican II and *Lingering Shadows*

Confronting institutional anti-Semitism: post-WWII

In the previous chapter, we noted that from 1944 to 1950 the Analytical Psychology Club in Zürich maintained a discretely concealed policy that limited the number of Jews who were permitted to join. When Aryeh Maidenbaum uncovered this fact in 1988, it sent shock waves through the Jungian community. Nevertheless, Thomas Kirsch reminds us that:

> From today's perspective such quotas are unconscionable, yet in that era they were the rule rather than the exception. Quotas, particularly against Jewish people, were operative in schools, colleges, universities, the workplace and social clubs, and lasted well into the 1950s in America and Europe.
>
> (Kirsch, 2000, p. 34)

Agreed. However, this episode of institutionalized anti-Semitism cannot be passed over lightly, because it was preceded and followed by several deeply disquieting developments. For example, Deirdre Bair informs us that in 1914, Emilii Medtner, a middle-aged Russian of German descent, a patient and then a family friend of Jung's, was convinced that Jung's shared his own rabidly anti-Semitic views, which he spouted at length during many hours of conversation. Bair casts some doubt on the truth of Medtner's claim, but makes it clear from the context that Jung – who was still furious with Freud, no doubt – did nothing to challenge, interrupt or interpret these anti-Semitic tirades. (Medtner later became a Jungian analyst!) This raises questions about how Jung advised his pupils and followers to address or interpret similar expressions of hatred or mistrust toward Jews. Then there were the various papers Jung published that dwelt on the alleged differences between the Aryan and the Jewish unconscious, his friendship and collaboration with Wilhelm Hauer and the many alarming and odious remarks and missteps made between 1933 and 1939, when he finally broke off all communication with the Nazis.

Granted, Jung opposed the introduction of the quota in 1936, when the issue first arose. But his opposition flagged, and he fell silent by 1944, when Toni Wolff and C.A. Meier's policy prevailed (for a time). Even when the policy was revoked in 1950, Toni Wolff continued to voice anti-Semitic sentiments – as an insult to the memory of her bereaved sister's beloved husband, no less! And remember, the revocation on the membership restriction and the acrimonious exchange between Wolff and her sister transpired three and four years *after* Jung's private apology to Rabbi Leo Baeck.[1]

Meanwhile, after WWII, Neumann continued to battle the shape-shifting and thinly veiled anti-Semitism among Jung's devoted followers, who opposed the publication of Neumann's work – and Neumann personally – on specious grounds. And Neumann, apparently, was the *only* Jew among Jung's close followers who really challenged him privately on this score. That being so, it is astonishing to reflect that the only non-Jewish Jungian who took a strong and principled stand *against* anti-Semitism in this era was the American author Phillip Wylie. Though not particularly insightful, his uncharacteristically frank approach to the issue in his book *Generation of Vipers* (Wylie, 1943) was one of this book's few redeeming features. To the best of my knowledge, Wylie's was the most widely read critique of anti-Semitism by a non-Jew in the USA circa WWII until Carey McWilliams little masterpiece, *A Mask for Privilege: Anti-Semitism in America* appeared five years later (McWilliams, 1948).[2]

That being said, it is also entirely true that the restriction on Jewish membership that prevailed in Zürich for a time was not an isolated incident. Far from it! Jews weren't wanted anywhere, and were denied entry almost everywhere, in this period of history. And it was never just a question of country clubs or universities. That was the least of it! As the 1930s wore on, most countries closed their doors to all but a handful of Jewish immigrants and refugees. The British even halted (legal) Jewish immigration to Palestine, in deference to the Mufti, whose bloody insurrection of 1936 might be construed as the very first *intifada*. Who knows how many of the 6 million who perished then would have survived had they been permitted to immigrate safely and legally to other shores? So on reflection, the actions of Wolff, Meier and their colleagues were merely a faint echo of the larger, global trends that engulfed the Jewish people.

That being said, while Jung and his circle were less than admirable in this regard, their attitudes, utterances and actions, though reprehensible, no doubt, were not in any way *unusual*, given the temper of the times. On the contrary, the whole of Christendom was institutionally anti-Semitic. Devout Christian leaders and activists who addressed the evils of anti-Semitism in a courageous and outspoken way – like Americans Dorothy Day or Reinhold Niebuhr, for example – were outliers, whose words were seldom heeded by their clerical establishments. This seems to be the gist of Adolf Guggenbühl-Craig's remark that:

> Everyone in Europe, with perhaps the exception of the Italians, was anti-Semitic in the last century, and in the centuries before that, as well as in this (20th) century. Anti-Semitism is part of the collective mythology, originating from the Christian religion. The Jews were considered to be killers of Christ.
>
> (Guggenbuhl-Craig, 1991 p. 342)

Though painful to contemplate, perhaps, this state of affairs explains why Germany and Austria's Churches – both Catholic and Protestant – capitulated to Hitler so quickly and completely in the wake of the Vatican's concordat with Hitler on July 20, 1933 (Heschel, 2008). Indeed, it was not until the Second Vatican Council, convened by Pope Paul VI, which ran from 1962 to 1965, that Catholic clergymen explicitly admonished the faithful that the Jews are not collectively responsible for the crucifixion, and started to address and reverse anti-Semitism in the Church. Though it commenced almost two decades after the Holocaust, Vatican II, as it is nowadays called, produced and encouraged much soul-searching and self-reflection among Christians, which significantly ameliorated – without actually eliminating – the anti-Semitic bias among Christian populations, including many Protestant denominations (Connelly, 2012).

Beginning in or around the mid-1960s – i.e. just after Vatican II – another cultural shift began. Up until then, the counter-cultural thrust of Jungian thought tilted away from the mainstream, to be sure, but in a decidedly conservative and anti-modernist direction (Ellwood, 1999; Sherry, 2010). This aristocratic bias, which Jung disavowed in his frequent claim to be "apolitical", is expressed in a particularly stark and disturbing form in a statement from his *Zarathustra* seminar of 1936. He wrote:

> The idea that every man has the same value might be a great metaphysical truth, yet in this space-and-time world it is the most tremendous illusion; nature is thoroughly aristocratic and it is the wildest mistake to assume that every man is equal. That is simply

not true. Anyone in his sound senses must know that the mob is just a mob. It is inferior, consisting of inferior types of the human species. If they have immortal souls at all then it is God's business, not ours, we can leave it to him to deal with their immortal souls which are presumably far away, as far away as they are in animals. I am quite inclined to attribute immortal souls to animals; they are just as dignified as the inferior man. That we should deal with the inferior man on our own terms is all wrong. To treat the inferior man as you would treat a superior man is cruel; worse than cruel, it is nonsensical, idiotic.

(Sherry, 2010, p. 94)

The idea that all human beings possess an immortal soul is a corollary of the idea that all human beings are made in God's image, which is an integral feature of both Jewish and Christian theology. It was never intended to erase or efface individual differences, or to deny the fact that people are born with differing levels of talent or ability, different temperaments and so on. Considered from an ethical (rather than metaphysical) standpoint, the belief in human equality merely means that regardless of their ability or circumstances, all people are entitled to be treated with dignity and respect – or as Immanuel Kant said, as ends in themselves, rather than as means to an end. However, even if we allow for a strong dose of polemical overstatement, in Jung's derisive handling of it, the belief in the fundamental equality of human beings – like the unity of the human species – is merely a ruse, an illusion contrived by the mob to promote mediocrity, just as Nietzsche claimed in *The Genealogy of Morals*.

That was Jung in 1936. But suffice it to say that in the 1960s, young people were increasingly interested in mythology, mandalas, yoga and varieties of religious experience that lay *outside* of mainstream churches. As a result of their increasing immersion in and attraction to Jungian ideas, the political center of gravity of the Jungian world gradually became more "extraverted", and shifted in a more progressive direction. This is reflected in the work of Andrew Samuels, for example, who wrote:

Whether we like it or not, depth psychology and politics are connected. As a recognition of that, we should consider expressly allying ourselves with marginal; and so called minority groups. We could contribute our limited but profound expertise to the achievement of their goals. Jung aligned himself with and sought power; we should align ourselves with the powerless. We could do this by using our analytical capacity to work on a clarification of the psychological experience of being a Jew, German, African American, homosexual, woman, man. We would assist such groups in getting behind the defensive stereotypes imposed by a threatened dominant culture as we explore the nature of differences itself.

(Samuels, 1991, p. 199)

Samuels' statement here was illustrative of the growing willingness to criticize Jung's reactionary politics, and an eagerness, in many cases, to execute a 180-degree turn away from Jung's reactionary conservatism. Of course, not everyone in the Jungian world repudiated the politics of the past, or acknowledged the merit of Samuels' critique. Many still clung to a conservative mindset. But as attitudes like his became more prevalent, and the Jungian movement grew to include larger numbers of people, the high-brow/low-intensity anti-Semitism so characteristic of Jung and his inner circle prior to WWII became even more muted than it was formerly. Even when it cropped up, as it did – and still does, occasionally – after 1965, the wider cultural milieu in which Jungians moved became less anti-Semitic than formerly. As a result, many Jews continued to train as Jungian analysts, though only a few had the stomach, the persistence or the historical awareness to dig deep into the movement's collective history and address these issues in their scholarly work.

Lingering Shadows

Among those who possessed these rare but important qualities were two Jewish Jungians, Aryeh Maidenbaum and Stephen Martin, who convened a conference at the New School for Social Research in New York City in 1989. The conference, called *Lingering Shadows: Jungians, Freudians and Anti-Semitism*, was cosponsored by the C.G. Jung Foundation for Analytical Psychology (New York), the Postgraduate Center for mental health, and the Union of American Hebrew Congregations. The purpose of the conference was (1) to lay to rest certain myths and misconceptions about Jung's anti-Semitism, while nevertheless (2) addressing Jung's "shadow involvement in relation to Nazism, totalitarianism and the real or imagined differences between 'Jewish psychology' and that of any other group or people", and finally (3) to do both of these things in the interests of facilitating more constructive and respectful dialogue between the followers of Freud and Jung, who, with rare exceptions, had shunned or disparaged one another ever since the great rupture of 1913. Maidenbaum and Martin felt that

Jungians should take the initiative in opening up this dialogue, because "to look into the darkness, personal or collective, was, in Jung's mind, the cornerstone of a psychologically authentic and ethical life" (Martin, 1991 p. 3).

The original impetus for *Lingering Shadows* came from Maidenbaum, an American-born Israeli, whose analyst and teacher, Dr. Rivkah Schaerf Kluger, had been a student and analysand of Jung's. Dr. Kluger reassured Maidenbaum that the rumors he'd heard about Jung being an anti-Semite and a Nazi sympathizer were without foundation. Nevertheless, once his analysis was concluded, Maidenbaum decided to revisit this issue in more depth, in the hopes of getting to the bottom of things. This prompted him and his friend Stephen Martin to collect materials and testimony that were pertinent to the issue, which had lain dormant for decades. In the process, they discovered that

> the literature on this subject ranges from idolatry to witch hunting, from those who felt Jung could do no wrong to those who blatantly condemned him without familiarizing themselves with the factual material.
>
> (Maidenbaum, 1991, p. x)

To their credit, Maidenbaum and Martin were determined to avoid these polarized and sterile extremes, and bring sober, scholarly scrutiny to bear on these vexing issues, which were – and to a lesser extent, still are – significant stumbling blocks to constructive intellectual engagement between Freudians and Jungians. The conference they convened for this purpose resulted in an edited anthology containing thought-provoking essays by many of Jung's students, and his students' students (or children), including Ernest Harms, James Kirsch, Richard Stein, Jay Sherry, Arthur Williamson, Geoffrey Cocks, Andrew Samuels, Paul Roazen, Ann Belford Ulanov, Michael Vanoy Adams, Werner Engel, Micha Neumann, Phillip Zabriskie, Jerome Bernstein, Marga Speicher, Adolf Guggenbühl-Craig and Thomas Kirsch.

Though these essays varied somewhat in subject matter, emphasis and perspective, the volume as a whole was a complete "game changer". We cannot summarize or review all of these papers separately, but several addressed issues that are immediately relevant to our line of inquiry, and worth noting, going forward. First, two historians, Arthur Williamson and Geoffrey Cocks, provided readers with much needed historical background to contextualize the other writers' more personal reflections – which, with the exception of Paul Roazen's thoughtful piece, all reflect their standing as Jungian "insiders". Williamson's piece, entitled "The Cultural Foundations of Racial Religion and Anti-Semitism" is a brilliant analysis of the religious roots of anti-Semitism and philo-Semitism in the post-Elizabethan world, with some intriguing reflections on apocalypticism, Christian Zionism, the Reformation, the Enlightenment, abolitionism, modernism and anti-modernism (Williamson, 1991). The main drawback here was that Williamson did not specifically mention Freud, Jung or depth psychology once in his essay, leaving the reader to "connect the dots", or make the necessary inferences about how these larger historical trends shaped the world in which the relationship and then the rupture between Freud and Jung took place.

By contrast, Geoffrey Cocks' much briefer history ignored these overarching historical trends, for the most part, focusing squarely on the early 20th-century and the philosophical differences between Freud and Jung, and on Jung's conduct from 1933 to 1940. His conclusion is noteworthy. He wrote:

> European anti-Semitism was not usually racist in the Nazi sense; rather the interwar fascist movement capitalized on a more general cultural movement against materialism that often caricatured Jews as lacking "spirituality" … Jung never expressed himself this way, but did share the widespread concern about the deterioration of spiritual values that, among other things, led him to see in the mass movements of the 1920s and the 1930s elements of what he called liberation. This philosophical stance cultivated degrees of anti-Semitism inherited from the culture, the intensity of which varied with time and event. *It must be said that Jung broke with these notions in a way that suggests a dialectic of prejudice and tolerance within him that was ultimately resolved in favor of the latter.*
> (Cocks, 1991, p. 164, emphasis added)

Clearly, Cocks' wanted to be fair and judicious, and was largely successful, given what was known at that time. However, he was not privy to correspondence between Kirsch and Jung, which only became available in 2011. There, Kirsch proposes (in 1934) that Jews are spiritually deficient because they rejected Jesus, and Jung concurs. Besides, after the appearance of Jung's correspondence with Kirsch, we gained access to Jung's *Red Book*, which Jung stopped working on in 1930. There, without any prompting from Kirsch, Jung also deemed Jews to be spiritually deficient.

Cocks had no way of knowing all this, to be sure. But he made a minor misstep here by suggesting – without intending to, I suspect – that Jung saw *all* the mass movements of that era as potentially liberating. That is not so. On the contrary, Jung thought that Nazism and neo-paganism were infused with abundant potential for spiritual renewal, but reviled Soviet Communism as an extreme embodiment of the "soulless materialism" he lamented as the scourge of modern Europe. And in fairness, it must be conceded that Freud – another representative of "soulless materialism" – was more prescient than Jung on this score. Freud regarded Communism and Fascism as equally totalitarian and barbaric movements based on illusions about race or about human nature in general (Freud, 1927).

James Kirsch's paper, entitled "Carl Gustav Jung and the Jews: The Real Story" addresses Jung's lapse of judgment here from a personal point of view. In May of 1933, Kirsch was convinced that Nazism would be catastrophic for the Jews, and for Europe generally, while Jung still cherished hopes that it would transform the world for the better, and reproached him for leaving Germany without cause. When Kirsch met up with Jung again in 1947, the first thing Jung did was to apologize for his earlier reproach and for some things he wrote at that time. Kirsch added:

> I regret very much that this apology was only made to me personally but was never put in public writings, so that one could see how Jung's opinions in regard to Jews changed between 1934 and 1947. Some people, disappointed by Jung's attitude, expected a public statement about his mistakes and some kind of clarification. He felt that his article "After the Catastrophe" (1945) was sufficient to state his position.
>
> (Kirsch, 1991, p. 64)

In fairness to Kirsch, Jung's attitude did change, and the scholarly consensus is that this process began in earnest after his second heart attack in 1946, one year before he and Kirsch were reunited. But was Jung's statement from the preceding year – "After the Catastrophe" – really sufficient? James Kirsch thought so, because he went on to say that Nazism was clearly

> a mass psychosis; it represented an outburst of the collective unconscious. As with his patients, Jung counted on the healing and creative forces inherent in the human psyche to do their work. He felt

justified in this attitude because, as he says, the contents of the collective unconscious are themselves, ambivalent.

(Kirsch, 1991, p. 84)

In other words, Kirsch said that Jung was ambivalent toward Nazism because the archetypes themselves are ambivalent, lending themselves to creative or destructive purposes. Reading between the lines, so to speak, Aryeh Maidenbaum sounded far less satisfied with Jung's public posture (p. 295). He related the story of Neumann's friend, Siegmund Hurwitz, who expressed to Jung how disturbed he was at the content and timing of "The State of Psychotherapy Today" (1934). Evidently, Jung replied: "Today I would not write this article in this way. I have written in my long life many books, and I have also written nonsense. Unfortunately, that was nonsense" (Maidenbaum, 1991 p. 295).

Reflecting on this exchange, Maidenbaum commented: "This was as close as we (Maidenbaum and Martin) could get to an acknowledgement by Jung that there was anything wrong with what he had written and published in that period" (p. 295).

What, if anything, can we learn from these accounts? James Kirsch regretted that Jung never apologized publicly, but then chastised Jung's critics for the misunderstandings that ostensibly led them to imagine that Jung was anti-Semitic. Indeed, he appeared to believe that if Jung had offered a more fulsome public apology, his critics would have been neutralized, and that he (Kirsch) would not have needed to leap to his defense, but that Jung's critics were nevertheless *more* responsible for this sorry state of affairs than Jung himself. Maidenbaum, by contrast, was also disappointed by Jung's reticence but mounted no defense of his analyst's analyst. Though not stated in so many words, Maidenbaum's attitude appears to be more skeptical, less forgiving than Kirsch's – as if to suggest that Jung really owed the Jewish people a public apology, and that his refusal to do so raises doubts about *his* motives, rendering the comments of some of his critics intelligible and perhaps warranted, in the circumstances.

Unfortunately, some effort and reflection are needed to tease out these subtle differences, because when all is said and done, neither Kirsch nor Maidenbaum risked being *overtly* critical of Jung's behavior on this score. The reason for this was probably alluded to (in a different context) by another Jewish analyst, Werner Engel, in his contribution to *Lingering Shadows*, entitled "Thoughts and Memories of C. G. Jung". Like Maidenbaum, Engel was analyzed by Rivkah Schaerf Kluger – albeit while she was still Rivkah Schaerf – and was on intimate terms with five of the most prominent German-Jewish Jungians – James Kirsch, Max Zeller, Gerhard Adler, Ernest Bernhard and Erich Neumann. He recalled having lengthy discussions with each of them on the subject of loyalty to Jung, noting that they were all loyal to Jung in their own ways, but that all felt moved to "acceptance of Jung as a total personality". I would venture to speculate that Maidenbaum and Martin, being second (or third) generation Jungians, probably felt this need (or pressure) less acutely; hence *Lingering Shadows*, which appeared almost three decades after Jung's death.

One of Maidenbaum and Martin's motives for launching their research was their desire to facilitate more frank and productive exchanges between Jungian analysts and their Freudian counterparts. That being so, permit me to point out the striking complementarity between these Jewish Jungians' loyalty to Jung, which was clearly central to their personal and professional identities, and the premium placed on fidelity to Freud among Freud's followers, especially those of the first and second generation. As Erich Fromm pointed out long ago, the demand for fidelity to Freud among the Freudian faithful led to an idealizing attitude and a defensiveness on Freud's behalf that engendered historiographical errors, omissions and distortions of almost Stalinist proportions (Burston, 1991). Jung himself was among the first victims of these trends – a fact most Jungians will readily acknowledge. But many of these same Jungians are loathe to acknowledge similar trends in the history and historiography of the Jungian field, or the fact that Christian churches in the pre-WWII era were institutionally anti-Semitic; a fact which, in powerful if indirect ways, shaped the latent (and occasionally, explicit) anti-Semitism of Jung's circle before, during and even after WWII.

Though seldom noted, there are important lessons to be learned from this curious state of affairs. The mutual incomprehension and mistrust between Freudian and Jungians that Maidenbaum and Martin lamented is based in no small part on the loyalty that members of each school felt toward their founders. Loyalty to Jung or fidelity to Freud were traits that first generation analysts typically exhibited and subtly cultivated in their (second generation) trainees, so that it often took several generations before these traits wore off or diminished in intensity, rendering real dialogue between the two approaches possible.

One ramification to this state of affairs was that while Jungians had an investment in denying or ignoring the institutionalized anti-Semitism of the Christian Churches, Freudians, by and large, had no stake in doing so. On the contrary, owing to Freud's well-known antipathy toward the Catholic Church, and to anti-Semites in general, Freudians' identification with and fidelity to Freud would likely push them in the *opposite* direction, fostering what Jung referred to as their "anti-Christianism".

That being said, the astonishing rise of short-term cognitive behavioral therapy (CBT) and Big Pharma in the final quarter of the 20th century has given Freudian, Jungians and indeed anyone committed to insight-oriented long-term psychotherapy a powerful incentive to drop the partisan poses of yesteryear and find common ground. And as a result, the mutual mistrust and misunderstanding between Freudians and Jungians will continue to dissipate somewhat with each passing decade, or at least as long as their treatment modalities remain largely unavailable (or simply unaffordable) to the general public.

Even so, the process initiated by Maidenbaum and Martin in 1989 is still far from complete. In 2002, psychoanalytic historian Paul Roazen published a book called *The Trauma of Freud: Controversies in Psychoanalysis*, the second chapter of which is devoted to Jung and the Zürich School. Roazen reminded Freudians of Jung's many contributions to psychoanalysis, and of their carefully cultivated amnesia concerning Jung's ideas and contributions. And he did a judicious job of reviewing recent literature on the relationship and falling out between Freud and Jung, including thoughtful books by Linda Donn, Peter Homans, Robert Hopcke, Anthony Stevens, J.J. Clarke, Richard Noll and Anthony Storr. His handling of Jung's anti-Semitism was honest, but awkward and tentative in places. For example, he confessed that he only participated in the *Lingering Shadows* conference after considerable inner turmoil. Unlike most psychoanalytic historians, Paul was extremely alert to the self-serving quality of much Jung-bashing in the Freudian world. Nevertheless, even he was forced to admit that

> speaking as a political scientist, the worst of what Jung wrote came in the early days of the rise to power of the Nazis in Germany. Further, Jung took the trouble to go there to deliver his message; he undertook to make political choices, for which he must historically be held responsible ...
>
> Jung seems to have been politically naïve, even stupid, though I must say that what often looks like stupidity can mask prejudice and conviction. In Jung's case it is not as if others in the field did not ... point out to him ... where he was going wrong.
>
> (Roazen, 2002, p. 40)

He concluded: "... as far as I know Jung never adequately acknowledged the full impropriety of his conduct" (p. 41), adding afterwards that

> some of Jung's ideas had enough echo in what he heard from Germany's Nazis for him to think that his work might fit in there. But to the extent that his work was opportunistically motivated, he is not going to come off well on this particular score.
>
> (Roazen, 2002, p. 42)

Much as I honor Paul's memory (Burston, 2020), "impropriety" was a strange word to use in this context. One's conduct can be quite improper, according to prevailing cultural codes of behavior, and yet be perfectly ethical. Indeed, to be genuinely ethical, one must often *be* "improper". Any fool knows that. Though I cannot prove it, of course, Roazen's use of the term "impropriety" in this context was probably a symptom of an ongoing inner struggle between his desire to be bluntly honest and his fear of giving offense unnecessarily. This curious conflictedness and the resulting lack of precision on his part actually speak in his favor, humanly speaking.

Finally, we come to the paper that Andrew Samuels, contributed to *Lingering Shadows*, entitled "National Socialism, National Psychology and Analytical Psychology". Written mere months before the fall of the Berlin Wall, and just two years before the collapse of the Soviet Empire, it was the only paper in this symposium that directly called attention to the recent resurgence of anti-Semitism in Hungary, Poland, Rumania, East Berlin and France – countries which have since undergone an even deeper and more worrisome resurgence of anti-Semitism, along with Russia, Western Europe and Scandinavia. Unlike Jung, whose *völkisch* habits of thought inclined toward a racialist essentialism, Samuels treated nations as mere social constructions that required (real or imaginary) Others to maintain a measure of self-definition. And like Roazen, Samuels insisted that psychology and politics can never be completely separated. Indeed, Samuels said:

> We may have to question the very way we work, for private practice with a privileged clientele is not politically neutral. Our way of working has affected our way of thinking. We may have to question our automatic preference for the inner world and our tendency to make "inner" and "outer" or "private" and "public" into polar opposites, rejecting multidisciplinary work as "unpsychological".
>
> (Samuels, 1991, p. 207)

Furthermore, he insisted

> there is no need to retreat behind the barrier of the "clinical". We need, I think, to sit down with the materially disadvantaged and the socially frightened, as well as with educated analysands. We should be engaged when a Law of Return is passed and small ethnic groups gain or regain their lands; hence we should be engaged when an *intifada* erupts. We *should* be concerned with promised lands as well as with sovereign nation-states; with the people as well as with their leaders.
>
> (Samuels, 1991, p. 206)

Samuels was clearly concerned about the Middle East situation, and his commentary raised a number of pertinent questions that we address in the forthcoming chapter. But one question that neither he nor the other contributors to *Lingering Shadows* addressed, which is still begging to be asked, finally, is: Is there a coherent Jungian theory of anti-Semitism, and if so, how do Jungians address anti-Semitism in the clinical setting? As anti-Semitism ramps up all around the world – as it has increasingly since Samuels' paper was published – how do Jungian clinicians understand and treat people who are on the giving or the receiving end of anti-Semitic prejudice? Given the astonishing paucity of literature on this subject, the answers to these questions – which basically remain unasked, let alone unanswered – are far from clear.

Second, what relevance does all this have for the Right of Return claimed by Jews and Palestinians alike with respect to the "Promised Land"? These issues, which Samuels raised, were never addressed by Kirsch or Neumann in their correspondence with Jung because nothing like a "right of return" was remotely conceivable before 1948. So, serious reflection on these matters requires that we revisit the relationships between Judaism, anti-Semitism, Zionism and anti-Zionism since the creation of Israel, which are ubiquitous in contemporary politics, and rethink our approach to issues that have lain (more or less) dormant in Jungian circles since in the early 1930s.

Notes

1 For two illuminating discussions of the Club's restrictions on Jewish membership, see Aryeh Maidenbaum's "Lingering Shadows: A Personal Perspective" and Jerome Bernstein's "Remarks for the Workshop on Jung's Anti-Semitism" in Lingering Shadows: Jungians, Freudians and Anti-Semitism (Maidenbaum and Martin, 1991).

2 Because it was a work of fiction, I am not counting Laura Z. Hobson's novel *Gentleman's Agreement* (Hobson, 1947) or the film of the same name starring Gregory Peck, directed by Elia Kazan.

References

Burston, D. 1991. *The Legacy of Erich Fromm*. Cambridge, MA: Harvard University Press.

Burston, D. 2020. *Psychoanalysis, Politics and the Postmodern University*. New York: Palgrave MacMillan.

Cocks, G. 1991. "The Nazis and C.G. Jung", in Maidenbaum, A. and Martin, S. 1991, *Lingering Shadows: Jungians, Freudians and Anti-Semitism*, New York: Shamabala, pp. 157–166.

Connelly, J. 2012. *From Enemy to Brother: The Revolution in Catholic Teaching on the Jews*. Cambridge, MA: Harvard University Press.

Ellwood, R. 1999. *The Politics of Myth*. Albany: SUNY Press.

Freud, S. 1927. *The Future of An Illusion*. Vol 21. Standard Edition. London: Hogarth Press.

Guggenbühl-Craig, A. 1991. "Reflections on Jung and Anti-Semitism" in *Lingering Shadows: Jungians, Freudians and Anti-Semitism*, New York: Shambala, pp. 341–348.

Heschel, S. 2008. *The Aryan Jesus: Christian Theologians and the Bible in Nazi Germany*. Princeton, NJ: Princeton University Press.

Hobson, L.Z. 1947. *Gentlemen's Agreement*. New York: Simon and Schuster.

Kirsch, J. 1991. "Carl Gustav Jung and the Jews: The Real Story" in *Lingering Shadows: Jungians, Freudians and Anti-Semitism*, New York: Shambala, pp. 51–88.

Kirsch, T. 2000. *The Jungians: A Comparative and Historical Perspective*. London: Routledge.

Maidenbaum, A. and Martin, S. 1991. *Lingering Shadows: Freudians, Jungians and Anti-Semitism*. New York: Shamabala.

Maidenbaum, A. 1991. "Lingering Shadows: A Personal Perspective", in *Lingering Shadows: Freudians, Jungians and Anti-Semitism*, New York: Shamabala, pp. 291–300.

Martin, S. 1991. Introduction to *Lingering Shadows: Freudians, Jungians and Anti-Semitism*, New York: Shambala, pp. 1–16.

McWilliams, C. 1948. *A Mask for Privilege: Anti-Semitism in America*. Boston: Little Brown and Company.

Roazen, P. 1991. "Jung and Anti-Semitism" in Maidenbaum, A. and Martin, S. 1991. *Lingering Shadows: Jungians, Freudian and Anti-Semitism*. New York: Shambala, pp. 211–222.

Roazen, P. 2002. "Jung and the Zurich School", in *The Trauma of Freud: Controversies in Psychoanalysis*. New Jersey: Transaction Press, pp. 15–46.

Samuels, A. 1991. "National Socialism, National Psychology and Analytical Psychology", in Maidenbaum, A. and Martin, S. 1991. *Lingering Shadows: Jungians, Freudians and Anti-Semitism*. New York: Shamabala, pp. 177–210.

Sherry, J. 2010. *C.G. Jung: Avant-Garde Conservative*. Cham, Switzerland: Palgrave MacMillan.

Williamson, A. 1991. "The Cultural Foundations of Racial Religion and Anti-Semitism", in Maidenbaum, A. and Martin, S. 1991. *Lingering Shadows: Jungians, Freudians and Anti-Semitism*. New York: Shamabala, pp. 135–156.

Wylie, P. 1943. *Generation of Vipers*. New York: Farrar and Rhinehart.

6 Sacred ground
Palestine, Israel and the Right of Return

Self-betrayal and "baptism"

As noted earlier, Kirsch and Neumann did agree on several important issues. They rejected Jung's contention that Jews have no culture of their own, and protested that the Hasidic and the Zionist movements attest to the vitality and creativity of the Jewish psyche. Similarly, they both stressed the originally introverted character of Jewish religiosity until the advent of the Enlightenment. However, they said, the promise of emancipation and full civic equality brought with it the dangers of assimilation, and the sudden erosion of the remarkable cohesion that characterized Jewish communities until then. From the late 18th century till the 1930s, for better or worse, Jewish communities simply *had* to become far more extraverted in order to adapt and "catch up" with their Christian counterparts, and this led to a sharp decline in the traditional uniformity of belief and conduct. As Neumann told Jung:

> With the advent of emancipation ... (the) collective bond disintegrates and, in a magnificent effort, the Jews attempt to catch up with the Occidental world in all areas, (which) led to an extraversion of such great magnitude that all libido was withdrawn from the inner world. This leads to complete "forgetting", to de-Semitization, to the disintegration into traditionlessness, to exceedingly isolated individuals without foundations, without cultural, historical or psychic continuity. This is the Jew you know.

Neumann then went on to add that the loss of the religious-collective foundation

> had then to and must now lead via rationalism, materialism and all the relevant childhood diseases ... (and was) accelerated by the fact

that at the same time the West was going through a corresponding phase ... positivism, science, technology that reinforced not insubstantially the illusory feeling of "brotherliness" between Jews and non-Jews.

(Liebscher, 2015, pp. 47–48)

With that said, however, on closer inspection, Kirsch and Neumann adopted fundamentally different stances toward Judaism and by implication, different stances toward Jung. For example, at the peak of his Zionist enthusiasm Kirsch claimed that Jews in the Galut (diaspora) were out of touch with God, and could only experience the Shekinah – (Hebrew for the Divine Presence which, unlike the Holy Spirit in Christianity, is personified as female) – in the Promised Land. This absurd proposition probably did nothing to endear him to residents of Tel Aviv – a famously secular city. Moreover, having abandoned Palestine for greener pastures less than two years later, he probably lived to regret this claim on other grounds. Similarly, Kirsch wrote to Jung that:

Jewish consciousness has the characteristic that ... something essential is missing; something suppressed lives in the Jewish soul, which induces even in the educated Jew the most peculiar affects and hysterical reactions.

(Lammers, 2011, p. 50)

Kirsch said that the "peculiar affects and hysterical reactions" that supposedly afflict the Jewish soul are attributable to the fact that the Jews rejected Jesus. In his reply, Jung expressed complete agreement. Perhaps it never occurred to these learned gentlemen that explaining a form of mental disorder that is prevalent in a given population by invoking a *theological* argument which attributes Jewish suffering to the Jews' own misdeeds many centuries before is rather strange behavior for men of science, especially since it implies that Jews cannot be spiritually or psychologically whole – according to their criteria – until they *do* accept Christ. (How convenient!) Indeed, it is particularly odd since there were so many more plausible explanations available to them, such as the intergenerational transmission of trauma,[1] or the obvious fact that the late nineteenth and early twentieth centuries were simply saturated with brutal pogroms all through Eastern Europe, which the Nazis were now itching to emulate (and exceed.)

Neumann learned of the agreement between Jung and Kirsch during his first visit to Kirsch's apartment in Tel Aviv in the summer of 1934.

Not only did Neumann reject this "explanation" for the traits that Kirsch described, he doubted their very existence. And in a handwritten addendum to a letter posted sometime in November of 1934, Neumann vigorously contested Jung's disparaging claim that the Biblical ban on idolatry is no different in meaning and no more important for the history of civilization than "an ancient tribal tradition" Jung had observed among an African tribe at Mt. Elgon, where he'd visited in 1925.[2]

Finally, it is worth noting that in a letter dated May 7, 1934, where Kirsch first expounded on the "Christ-complex", lamenting that Jews made a "vital mistake" in rejecting Jesus, he addressed Jung as follows:

> we are not nomads, but a restless people that has lost its living God, despite all the warnings of the prophets
>
> You are not the first, and will not be the last, whose warnings we cast aside. But I believe that – especially at this moment – your way will lead us back to the Living One and may be of enormous significance for the rebirth of the Jews.
>
> (Lammers, 2011, p. 43)

In other words, he was casting Jung in the role of a latter day prophet; someone divinely inspired who can help Jews recover their connection to God. Contrast this statement of Kirsch's with Neumann's frequent complaints (in the same period of time) that Jung was ignorant of (or indifferent to) the history and culture of the Jewish people.

Other examples could be provided, but the overall pattern is now quite clear. Kirsch made significant concessions to Jung's anti-Semitic biases, while hailing him as a prophet. By contrast, Neumann regularly pushed back against them, albeit only in private or the presence of colleagues, never in public or in print. Moreover, to the best of my knowledge, he never risked his relationship to Jung by *directly* accusing him of being anti-Semitic, though he criticized several of Jung's followers along these lines. Nevertheless, Neumann conveyed his distaste for Kirsch's sycophantic posture (and his anger toward Jung for tolerating or encouraging it) in a rather harsh remark about another Jewish Jungian, Heinz Westmann, in a letter from October 29, 1935, when he reminded Jung:

> You did express to me once your abhorrence toward this phenomenon of self-betrayal but I have not noticed anywhere that you have tangibly nailed it down. Please do not misunderstand this to be impudence; as a question this is important to me. I don't know if you are familiar with Westmann's lecture, which, by the way, is in many ways very interesting, but it makes *me* howl with pity. Clueless

in things Jewish ... (he) ... puts himself forward as a Jewish representative but this is a "convert" in the simple sense of the word. As
has become evident to me though, individuation does not belong to
the category of confession but to that of growth.

(Liebscher, 2015, pp. 116)

Though it wasn't stated openly, the sub-text here is that, in Neumann's
view, Jung did not notice or simply did not mind acts of self-betrayal by
Jews who champion his cause, and that he may be mistaking a strongly
sympathetic familiarity with his ideas with actual individuation. It is
hard to imagine Jung tolerating this kind of comeuppance from any
of his other Jewish followers. I take this as a measure of Jung's respect
for Neumann's courage, and his acknowledgement of Neumann's
many gifts.

Meanwhile, after leaving Palestine and relocating in London, then
Los Angeles, Kirsch continued to drift toward Christianity, albeit
without actually converting. In a letter dated December 10, 1952, Kirsch
related a recent visit to the Cathedral of Strasbourg, where he saw a
depiction of the conquered synagogue and the Church Triumphant,
above which was a depiction of Mary being coronated by Christ. He
told Jung that he was deeply moved by this monument to Christian triumphalism, which is inextricably intertwined with anti-Semitism historically. And on December 28 of that same year, he wrote saying that: "I
can fully accept that Christ is 'the only begotten one' if Christ is also
an eternal mystery and ... a unique historical event", adding that he
also embraces the doctrine of Original Sin, which is incompatible with
Jewish teaching, but strikes him as "a prerequisite and a given in the
process of individuation" (Lammers, 2011, p. 155). Finally, on February
21, 1960, he wrote to Jung that

My greatest difficulty and also my greatest fear concerns the Jews.
They have, as the New Testament declares, always killed their
prophets. Not that I would like to be a prophet, but without fail I
have to deal with things sacred.

(Lammers, 2011, p. 264)

The perennial reproach favored by Christian and Muslim anti-Semites,
namely, that the Jews invariably kill their own prophets, sounds strange
coming from a Jewish man's lips. But perhaps Kirsch was merely
echoing the "party line"; one shared, for example, by Toni Wolff and
perhaps Jung himself. However, on reflection, the sub-text here appears
to be that, on some level, Kirsch really *did* want to be a prophet – a

status he formerly assigned to Jung – but feared that his seminars and publications, which were increasingly infused with Christian piety, would antagonize the Jewish community, and arouse murderous feelings against him.

Reading Kirsch and Neumann's letters to Jung, and Jung's replies to them, the cumulative impression one gets is that Jung valued Neumann's courage and originality, but nevertheless saw the gradual Christianization of educated and assimilated Jews (like Kirsch) through his Analytical Psychology Clubs as a good and necessary thing; something to be encouraged, rather than frowned on or questioned. Indeed, Jung could probably have spared Neumann a good deal of unnecessary suffering simply by owning up to this state of affairs. As it was, however, this remained a hidden agenda; an implicit (but taken for granted) feature of Jungian associations. Neumann's refusal (or inability) to play along caused him considerable inner and interpersonal conflict with Jung's followers in Zürich after WWII. Despite prodigious expenditures of time and energy, all efforts to mend the breach between them failed, finally. In 1959, in a scathing letter to Aniela Jaffé, Neumann conveyed his disappointment quite clearly, writing:

> You know, I put up with some things from C.G. that I am still amazed at today, but at least I know who he is in spite of this in relation to me. I do not have the feeling that the same is required of me from the Zürichers.
>
> (Liebscher, 2015, p. liv)

That being said, Kirsch and Neumann probably represent two polar extremes. None but Neumann put up such strenuous and principled resistance to this tacit drift toward Christianization, and few but Kirsch went quite so far in the other direction. This left poor Neumann morally and emotionally isolated, like Job among his clueless, self-righteous accusers. As he wrote to Jung in 1934:

> Analytical psychology, not yet fully realized, also holds this danger – that of the betrayal of one's own foundation in favor of a "nicer", "more advanced" and "more modern" one … It stands to reason that (the adoption of) … the "up to date" point of view of the individual of the Christian West, (represents) a psychological correspondence with baptism.
>
> (Liebscher, 2015, p. 115)

Zionism, the soil and the kibbutz movement

And what of Zionism? Both Kirsch and Neumann expressed the hope that they would contribute to the renewal of Jewish cultural life by reconciling Zionism with analytical psychology somehow. Yet despite their high hopes and lofty aspirations, both Kirsch and Neumann failed in the attempt, and were disappointed and dismayed shortly after their arrival in Palestine. Living in Tel Aviv, which was thronged with immigrants from diverse class and ethnic backgrounds, who spoke dozens of different languages, who practiced Judaism earnestly, half-heartedly or not at all, and who held widely divergent political views, they wondered when (or sometimes, even if) the Zionist project would cohere. Neumann at least took consolation in the thought that a new and vibrant Jewish culture would emerge in the next generation. However, neither Kirsch nor Neumann showed much interest in the kibbutz movement, which for all practical intents and purposes, was the backbone of the Zionist movement at the time. And Kirsch abandoned the Zionist project when he departed Tel Aviv. Neumann, by contrast, was determined to stay. On October 29, 1935, he said:

> The final problem in Judaism cannot be affected, it seems to me, and not theorized. I for one must realize it in a Jewish reality, as filthy and beautiful as it is and will be.
>
> (Liebscher, 2015, p. 116)

Further below, he added:

> The relationship of Jews to the "earth" is, in a fundamental way, the same as for the Gentiles and the Christians on a Gentile basis, but this problem can be resolved neither by a simple return to the soil (political Zionism) nor by only a psychical return to the soil (the Galut Jew with analytical psychology.) Both of these *must be achieved together.* The environment of the Jew in Europe is the collective unconscious of the non-Jew, and with this, his individuation is impossible. Only among Jews was it, and is it possible ... All these problems keep me occupied and will not allow me respite from this incessant work.
>
> (Liebscher, 2015, p. 117, emphasis added)

Jung responded (on December 22, 1935), saying that Neumann's conviction that Palestinian soil is essential to individuation is "very valuable to me". Nevertheless, he asked "How does the fact that the Jew in general has lived in other countries than in Palestine *for much longer* relate to this? Even Moses Maimonides preferred Cairo ..." This reply and the accompanying question can be interpreted in various ways, of course. Was Jung unaware that Maimonides' decided to settle in Cairo because Jerusalem's economy was shattered, rendering him unable to support his family there? Or was this a tactful, indirect way of expressing skepticism about Neumann's position? Or was it simply an expression of honest perplexity? Perhaps all of the above, in some measure? We'll never know for sure. In any case, it is doubtful that Jung gave Neumann's anguished reflections on this matter much attention after this exchange, when Neumann himself became deeply preoccupied with other matters. This change in priorities did not necessarily alter Neumann's basic position, or the commitments that flowed from it. But the whole question, which seemed urgent at the time, subsided into relative obscurity as the world lurched inexorably toward WWII.

And so now the question arises, how do *we* understand or address Neumann's position today? Is it possible for Jews to individuate in the diaspora? Unlike Jung and Neumann, I doubt that direct contact with the soil is a potent factor in individuation one way or another. Indeed, the argument that it is a vital precondition for individuation *anywhere* strikes me as implausible. I am inclined to believe that individuating as a Jew is easier in the midst of other Jews; that the drift to assimilation and the loss of cultural memory increases dramatically when the languages, the literature, the humor and traditions of the Jewish people are largely absent from the life of the individual. Where this cultural disconnection happens is less important in the long run. Why?

Let us be frank, shall we? At the end of the day, dirt is dirt, and no portion of the earth's topography is *intrinsically* sacred. Nevertheless, human beings can relate to the soil in one of three fundamental ways. We can exhaust and deplete the soil, rendering it increasingly lifeless, or alternatively, we can render it more productive, and more conducive to supporting diverse forms of microbial, plant and insect life. The former approach is mere resource extraction for the sake of immediate profit, and requires no more than possession of the appropriate technology and a numb indifference to the welfare of other life forms and future generations of humankind who will depend on the soil's fertility. By contrast with resource extraction, the second mode of relatedness requires a profound libidinal investment, one that (literally) enlivens the soil. This way of relating to the soil fosters an awareness of the intricate interdependence of organic life forms, i.e. a reverence for life, and a sense of a connection with other organisms and for preceding generations, to whom our libido is also attached, the memory of whom still stirs feelings of gratitude and loss – in other words, reverence for the dead, our dearly departed, whose bodies have returned to the soil that sustained them, and that now sustains us and our children in turn. This kind of relationship to "mother earth" also builds a strong sense of community among those who share this mode of life and these sensibilities.

A third form of land use entails a sense of land-ownership in a purely commercial or proprietary sense. Here land is viewed as an asset or a commodity, and therefore a means to other ends. The real goal may be wealth, power or security, or some combination of these, depending on the landowner and his circumstances. But it does not entail a libidinous relationship or connection to the land, because the person's libido is invested elsewhere.

Now, as far as we know, these three modes of relatedness to the soil are all specifically human, but the libidinous mode of relatedness to the soil is more "natural" than the other two in the sense that it precedes them, in terms of cultural and historical development, binding the individual to previous and future generations, addressing our need for "roots", thereby enabling us to experience our individual lives as part of an intergenerational flow, rather than some absurd cosmic accident. So, soil is rendered sacred, not by its location or any intrinsic properties, but by the amount of libido invested in its cultivation or protection by members of a group. Similarly, a sacred place becomes hallowed ground because an ancestor or religious leader whose teaching confers a sense of collective identity on his (or her) followers walked or worshipped there, was buried there, or experienced something extraordinary – a "revelation" – that has come to inform (and in some sense define) the group's sense of being-for-itself.

Though they may not contribute to the process of individuation – and may indeed hinder it, in some respects – these (individual and collective) libidinal ties to the soil are not trivial. On the contrary, they run deep, and their loss or attenuation can be extremely wrenching and traumatic, and have long-standing intergenerational effects. That is why diaspora Jews' lingering attachment and attraction to the Promised Land was not an irrelevant factor in their psychology or their culture. For centuries after their dispersion in the second century, the liturgy and literatures of the Jewish people reaffirmed a "sacred tie" to the lands of Israel and Judea. Meanwhile, with rare exceptions, Jews were deprived of opportunities to relate to the soil *anywhere* in this fashion. In the absence of a libidinous relationship to the land, as Kirsch and Neumann correctly discerned, the study of Torah and the observance of Halakah became the "glue" that bound Jewish communities and generations together across space and time.

Unfortunately, the Enlightenment and the industrial age, and the arrival of opportunities to assimilate shattered that state of affairs for Jews who wanted to live in the modern world free of ancient impediments and superstitions holding them back, or alienating them from their (non-Jewish) neighbors. These were Jews like Heine, Freud and Einstein – men whose gifts and accomplishments were recognized far outside Jewish circles.

The problem was that in Western Europe, the backlash against Jewish emancipation was fierce, and getting increasingly violent with each passing decade. In Eastern Europe, where emancipation proceeded more slowly (or not at all), Jews were becoming increasingly radicalized (i.e. revolutionary and left-wing) and determined to escape or, whenever possible, fight back against their oppressors.

The Jews of Eastern and Western Europe finally united under the banner of Zionism because despite all the fancy talk about progress and the splendid good intentions of some tolerant and friendly folk, they knew that they would always be the victims of hatred and persecution in Christian and Muslim lands. Therefore, Zionism was defined as the movement of Jewish "auto-emancipation", and presupposed a collective effort to create a "safe space" for Jews to live together free of persecution (Avineri, 1981; Elon, 2002; Lacquer, 2006).

The kibbutz movement, which formed the backbone of the Zionist movement in the interwar period, was a "back to the land" movement inspired by the communitarian socialism of Moses Hess. It was notable for inventing a new mode of relatedness to the soil – one which recovered the old intimacy, the sense of "hallowed ground", minus the encumbrances of traditional-agrarian societies, namely slavery and feudalism, which deform the human spirit. After all, early agrarian societies were basically egalitarian, but as they grew in size, they gave rise to city states and empires that relied on slave labor to plant, tend and harvest crops. Alternatively, indigenous populations who relied on farming were often conquered by neighboring tribes or peoples, who became their lords and masters, while they became commoners, like those whom the Rabbis called Am Ha'Aretz (literally, the people of the earth).[3] As empires grew in size and sophistication, their aristocracies lost some or most of the libidinal attachment to the land that their subjects still experienced. In such cases, territorial expansion was often sought primarily for the sake of self-aggrandizement, or personal power and glory, not to nourish loved ones, or to benefit the lives of their subjects.

What on earth does this have to do with Jung, Kirsch, Neumann and Zionism? Patience, please. Remember, first, that when empires based on slavery collapsed, they tended to give way to feudal arrangements with tenant farmers cultivating the land for the benefit of their lords. Conditions of life for serfs and indentured servants were somewhat variable, but usually quite miserable, though in every instance where a hereditary aristocracy or land-owning class was established, there were also gender hierarchies, and a strict division of labor between the sexes.

In 1917, when the British issued the Balfour Declaration, announcing their intention of creating a Jewish homeland in what is now Israel, the majority of the Arabs living in Palestine consisted of families of tenant farmers, many of whom had tilled the soil there for centuries. By contrast, the *halutzim* (Hebrew for pioneers) who founded kibbutzim combined a loving intimacy with the soil with a conscious pursuit of Enlightenment ideals of equality, attempting to eliminate caste, class and gender inequality. In addition to being strange and outlandish to their new neighbors, their ambitions in this regard were also quite foreign to Jung, whose *völkisch* ideas about rootedness, authenticity and the people's relationship to the soil were infused with neo-feudal nostalgia, and a belief in the necessity of maintaining social (and/or racial) hierarchies – this being the reason he was attracted to Nazism, initially.

But as a consequence of the preceding, the kibbutz movement's aspirations were *also* somewhat foreign to urban intellectuals like Kirsch and Neumann, who claimed that contact with the land was vital, but never got their proverbial hands dirty. Moreover, perhaps, Neumann and Kirsch both believed that individuation – and by implication, wholeness and authenticity – requires an immersion in the collective unconscious, and by implication, the Jewish people's religious inheritance. But most kibbutzniks were devoutly secular in outlook, and associated piety, prayer and mysticism with Europe, oppression and the Yiddish language; in short, with archaic cultural adaptations that left Jews acutely vulnerable and generally despised by their non-Jewish neighbors. Accordingly, despite their love of the land, which was movingly conveyed in their poetry and song, the *halutzim* deemed religiosity to be irrelevant to the new, egalitarian, Hebrew-speaking culture slowly taking shape in the emerging Jewish homeland. They were also, by dint of necessity, collectivistic in terms of their *modus vivendi*. Neumann's reservations about Zionism clearly hinged on this issue. In a handwritten addendum to an undated letter posted toward the end of 1934, he wrote to Jung that:

> there is a danger of a neo-orthodoxy, a communist collectivism and revisionist nationalism. Therefore, it seems to me that by means of the neuroticizing individualization and rationalization of assimilation a compensatory counteraction was set in motion in the form

of regenerating Zionism. (Activation of the archetypal symbols: Return – returning home to oneself – rebirth.) The danger exists that one will undo the individualization process that I regard as the historically necessary action of the emancipation and will lurch into this regeneration movement, head over heels, without any personal processing of it.

(Liebscher, 2015, pp. 62–63)

If one were to judge from this statement alone, it would appear that Neumann was more concerned with the prospect of de-individualization that Kibbutz life presented than he was impressed with their community and nation building potential. A little further below, Neumann adds that

the protestantization of Judaism seems to me to be necessary despite its collective ambitions. For me, Palestine is in this regard only a sort of transition because individuation seems to require, even for a people, the responsible and critical engagement with the reality of the world

(Leibscher, 2015, p. 64)

The tacit implication of these remarks is that the collectivism of the kibbutzim represents a regressive flight from reality, rather than a "critical engagement" with it. This probably accounts for the paucity of reflection in Neumann's correspondence on the kibbutz movement. Nevertheless, the kibbutz movement's embrace of Enlightenment values meant that men and women – most of whom, like Abraham, left their families and countries of origin voluntarily – were afforded equal educational and vocational opportunities, and played an equal role in the governance of these newly founded communities. It also meant an end to arranged marriages and greater freedom (for both sexes) to engage in premarital – or for that matter, extra-marital – sex if they wished.

Needless to say, though they shared a deep attachment to the soil, it is hard to imagine a more profound mismatch in lifestyle and sensibilities than the one between kibbutzniks and their Arab neighbors, who were (mostly) religious Muslims who adhered to traditional-feudal norms and customs and patriarchal-clan-based forms of governance.[4] This was not a subject that either Kirsch or Neumann addressed. Palestinian peasants were doubly resentful of these brash European interlopers because they typically bought land from wealthy Arab landowners; men whose proprietary attitude toward the land enabled them to part happily with their property, which they regarded as a commodity, a means to other ends. Initially, the tracts of land purchased from Arab landowners were mostly desert and swamps that were sparsely inhabited; land considered of little value, and useless for agricultural cultivation, which was gradually reclaimed and revivified through ingenuity and hard work. But as time wore on, good arable soil was often purchased as well, and when this happened, tenant farmer families, some of whom had dwelt on the land for centuries, were displaced to make way for Jews to settle. As historian Benny Morris points out, neither the Jewish settlers who purchased this land nor the Arab land owners who sold it to them demonstrated concern for the welfare of displaced tenant farmers and their families (Morris, 2001).

As a result, Arab discontent mounted, and was already evident in 1917, when the British unveiled the Balfour Declaration, i.e. long before Kirsch and Neumann arrived on the scene. The Zionist response was twofold. One the one hand, there was *Brit Shalom* (lit. "covenant of peace"), a small but influential group founded in 1925, led by Achad Ha'Am, Judah Magnes, Martin Buber, Gershom Scholem, Ernst Simon and Henrietta Szold, who sought to create a thriving cultural and economic hub for Jews in Palestine, but *without* contesting Arab and Palestinian sovereignty over the land. They were willing to negotiate restrictive quotas on Jewish immigration for the sake of peace and the cessation of violence. Though less flexible on the issue of immigration quotas, perhaps, the Kibbutz Artzi movement also sought to create conditions for shared sovereignty and neighborly coexistence, and unlike Brit Shalom, which disbanded in 1942, continues in that effort to this day (Avineri, 1981).

At the other extreme were Vladimir Jabotinsky (1880–1940) and the "Revisionist" school of Zionism, a militant Right wing faction that vigorously opposed any sort of quotas on Jewish immigration, and hoped to eventually expel all of the Palestinian inhabitants of Galilee, the West Bank and Gaza, by force if necessary. Jabotinsky, a gifted orator and playwright, was born and educated in Odessa, and together with Joseph Trumpeldor (1880–1920), founded the Jewish Legion that fought alongside the British in WWI. He also founded Jewish self-defense organizations, including *Betar*, *Hatzohar* and also the *Irgun*, whose young leader, Menachem Begin (1913–1992), eventually went on to become Prime Minister of Israel from 1977 to 1983. The Irgun was basically a terrorist organization that was quite separate from the Haganah, or the Jewish defense force, although they fought alongside the Haganah in 1948. Jabotinsky, Begin's mentor, was an ardent admirer of Benito Mussolini, who only severed his organizational ties with Italian Fascism when Mussolini acceded to pressure from Hitler to enact "race laws" in 1938 (Morris, 2001).

The Mufti, Palestinian resistance and the right of return

Meanwhile, between 1927 and 1929, friction between Jews and Muslims reached a boiling point on the Temple Mount, the site of the Wailing Wall and the Al-Aqsa mosque. The Wailing Wall is Judaism's holiest place, while the Al-Aqsa mosque, which lies directly above it, is Islam's third holiest site. Muslims accused the Jews of encroaching on and defiling their holy ground, and of wanting to destroy the Al-Aqsa mosque to rebuild their Temple, while Jews complained of being incessantly harassed, beaten and otherwise molested. They demanded unfettered access to the Wall. In the ensuing riots, hundreds of Jews and Muslims died, and many more were severely injured. A commission led by Sir Walter Shaw issued a report on the controversies that sparked these events, which were nominally about the control and administration of holy sites, but in a deeper sense, were emblematic of the conflicting agendas and aspirations of Palestinian Muslims and Jews.

In 1933, the year Hitler came to power, and Kirsch emigrated to Palestine, the most powerful member of Husseini clan, Mohammed Amin al-Husseini (1897–1974), the Mufti of Jerusalem, met with the German Consul General, Heinrich Wolff, to gauge the Nazis willingness to assist Palestinians in getting rid of the British and Jewish settlers. More than any single individual, the Mufti led the resistance to Zionism and Jewish immigration to Palestine between 1920 and 1939, orchestrating bloody uprisings in Jerusalem, Hebron, Petach Tikvah and Rosh Pina in 1920–1921, 1929 and 1936–1939 (Morris, 2001).

Some have said that the Mufti's alliance with Hitler was merely a tactical alliance, a matter of political expediency – that he was anti-Zionist and an Arab nationalist, but not actually an anti-Semite. Nonsense! (Johnson, 2010). The Jews that were massacred in Hebron were merely Yeshiva students, religious Jews. They weren't even Zionists. And after WWII, the Mufti personally insured that *The Protocols of the Elders of Zion* – a slanderous fabrication he cited at length in his testimony to the Shaw Commission– was translated into numerous languages spoken in the Muslim world, and was circulated widely. As a result, millions of Muslims alive today believe this lurid conspiracy theory is an authentic historical document which "proves" the existence of a worldwide Jewish conspiracy to dominate the world.

In any case, in 1937, after a secret meeting with Adolf Eichmann in Cairo, the British issued a warrant for the Mufti's arrest, and he fled to Beirut, Damascus, Baghdad, Tehran, then to Rome in 1940, and finally, in 1941, to Berlin, where he spent the remainder of WWII. In Rome and Berlin, the Mufti made numerous radio broadcasts to his followers and admirers back home, urging them to welcome the Nazis as liberators and turn on the British and the Jews. Moreover, with Eichmann's assistance, the Mufti organized a contingent of Bosnian Muslims to join the Waffen SS *Einsatzgruppen* in their campaign to slaughter Jews in the Balkans during the war, killing at least 20,000 (Morris, 2001).

Looking back, it is sobering to reflect that the Mufti, the first leader of the Palestinian resistance, was not merely a bystander or cheerleader during the Holocaust. He was an active perpetrator as well, and was widely admired by many Arab and Palestinian leaders. After WWII ended, al-Husseini took up residence in Cairo, where he assisted many high-ranking officers from the Wehrmacht to escape Allied justice by fleeing to Latin America, or else converting to Islam, acquiring new names and identities, and going "underground" (Johnson, 2010, pp. 110–113).

In 1947, the United Nations (UN) mandated the creation of two states in Palestine – one majority Jewish, one majority Arab – i.e. a two state solution, in Resolution 181. Had this plan been adopted, Jerusalem would have become an "international" city under UN protection and governance. The Jews accepted the international community's proposal. The Palestinian leadership and the surrounding Arab states did not, and declared war on the nascent Jewish state. In the lead up to the war, the Mufti tried to assert leadership over all the Arab forces dispatched from Cairo, Amman, Beirut, Damascus and Baghdad. His efforts failed. Despite being severely outnumbered and poorly equipped, the various Zionist groups joined forces to defeat these hostile forces with the help of returning WWII veterans. In the process, they seized additional territories (over and above those previously purchased or granted them by the UN) for the sake of maintaining defensible borders. The Mufti then decamped to Gaza where he, his family and a few other members of the (former) Palestinian ruling-class established the *All-Palestine Government*, which President Nasser dissolved in 1959, probably because of the Mufti's close ties with the Muslim Brotherhood, of which Hamas, which governs Gaza today, is an offshoot (Johnson, 2010).

Estimates vary somewhat, but in 1949, the UN issued a report which stated that in the course of the first Arab–Israeli conflict – which Israelis call the War of Independence, and Palestinians refer to as the Nakbah (Arabic for "the catastrophe") – some 726,000 Palestinians fled their homes, businesses and farms. That same year, 1949, the Mufti's government in Gaza and the entire Arab League demanded the prompt return of these refugees to their homes, and compensation for whatever losses they sustained in the course of this struggle. Significantly, however, they did not make this demand in the context of a peace proposal, nor did they recognize Israel as a sovereign state. On the contrary, while some Arab countries reluctantly signed armistices with Israel, their leaders were already talking publicly about waging the next anti-Zionist war. In other words, Israel was victorious for the time being, but still effectively under siege. Needless, to say, the Israeli government refused to consider repatriation of Palestinian refugees in circumstances like these. Their counter-offer, to repatriate 100,000 Palestinians in the event that a peace deal was struck, was also dismissed out of hand (Schwartz and Wilf, 2020).

Seventy years have elapsed since these events took place, and many, if not most Palestinians are still demanding a right of return to their former homes. Indeed, they demand that surviving refugees *and* their lineal descendants be returned and compensated for their losses. That being so, it is instructive to note that according to Al-Jazeera and Ma'an, the Palestinian Authority's news service, the number of Palestinian refugees and their lineal descendants worldwide numbered roughly 12.4 million in 2017. That is roughly six and a half times the number of Palestinians alive during the Nakbah.

Unfortunately, when discussing the Palestinian claim for a right of return, few people nowadays are willing or able to acknowledge the fact that from 1940 to 1974, some 850,000 Jews were *also* forcibly exiled from their ancestral homes in North Africa and the Middle East. They hailed from Baghdad, Damascus, Aleppo, Alexandria, Cairo, Sanaa, Tunis, Algiers, Tripoli and Rabat, where Jews had often settled well before the arrival of Christian missionaries of the first and second centuries, let alone the Muslim conquerors in the seventh century. Why the widespread reluctance to address this fact? Perhaps because many Jews in the Muslim world who wanted to co-exist peacefully with their neighbors (and maintain their traditional dhimmi status) suffered grievously for crimes they did not commit (Julius, 2020). Indeed, their only crime was that they were Jewish. It also complicates the prospects for peace in the Middle East exceedingly, because by and large, the lineal descendants of these Mizrahi Jews know that the Arab states will never compensate them for any of *their* losses, and are vehemently opposed to the return of the Palestinians.

So, finding a path to peace in the Middle East is devilishly difficult, because there is no trust between these bitter adversaries. Moreover, on close inspection, both the Zionist and the Palestinian narratives about the events of 1948 have been carefully curated to highlight injustices committed against Jews and Palestinian respectively, while simultaneously minimizing, distorting or willfully omitting evidence of the gravity or severity of crimes these peoples have committed *against each another* (Flapan, 1987; Morris, 2001). But while hardly innocent of human rights abuses – some dating back to 1947, when the UN (including the USSR) first mandated the creation of a Jewish homeland – the scale and severity of Israel's human rights abuses are dwarfed by the abuses routinely committed by neighboring Arab regimes in the same interval of time against their own people and against non-Muslim minorities – Ba'hai, Druze, Bedouin, Kurds, Parsees, Yazidis, and Maronite, Orthodox, Assyrian, Armenian and Coptic Christians. All of these faith communities were victims of vicious persecution in Arab and Muslim lands throughout the 20th century. (Remember the Armenian genocide?)

That being said, in the current political climate, the Palestinian narrative is winning far more hearts and minds in the West than it did in the mid-20th century. Indeed, in certain activist circles, the mere suggestion that Palestinians also committed serious crimes or injustices against Jews in British controlled Palestine, or after the establishment of the state of Israel, is deemed ridiculous (if not extremely offensive) because (1) Israel currently has the upper hand both economically and militarily and (2) many movement activists now equate Zionism with racism or White Supremacy, and/or treat it as a straightforward instance of (White) settler colonialism, which was designed from the outset to rob the indigenous population of their lands, their livelihoods, their dignity and their future. From their perspective, Islamist organizations – like Hamas and Hezbollah – that are sworn to Israel's destruction have a legitimate grievance with Israel and the West, even if they disagree with their methods.

For example, in June 2020, *Psychologists for Social Responsibility* (PsySR) issued a statement called "Psychologists in Solidarity with Palestine" in support of the *Boycott, Divest and Sanction* (BDS) movement, founded in 2005 by Omar Barghouti (1964–). Barghouti fervently opposes a two state solution, arguing that Jews and Muslims should live side by side as "equals" in a single, secular and democratic state called Palestine. However, he supports the Palestinians' right of return, while opposing similar rights for Jews, and freely acknowledges that this asymmetrical privilege would make Jews a minority almost immediately.

The statement issued by PsySR describes BDS as a nonviolent resistance movement inspired by the South African anti-apartheid movement which "... does not target identity. It strictly targets companies and institutions based on complicity in denying Palestinian rights". Furthermore, says this statement, BDS aims to dismantle Israel's continued egregious encroachment and theft of Palestinian land that displaces Palestinians into an increasingly more segregated space described as the "world's largest open-air prison." The situation constitutes as one of psychological, ethnic, and cultural genocide.

Then toward the end, the statement reads:

We call on peoples and organizations everywhere ... to stand in solidarity with Palestinian civil society's call for BDS against all organizations that are complicit in the devastating colonial-settler enterprise.

Now, in fairness, PsySR have played an exemplary role of championing progressive causes and anti-racist movements in the United States over the years. Nor are they alone among organizations of mental health professionals who support BDS or advocate on behalf of the Palestinian people. While I hasten to acknowledge the injustice of "Israel's ... egregious encroachment and theft of Palestinian land" since the Six Day War, and applaud the BDS movement's commitment to nonviolence, I strongly dispute the claim that Israel is committing "genocide" and that Zionism is essentially a "colonial-settler" enterprise.

There are several problems with these characterizations. First, with respect to the charge of genocide, consider the following. While the population of Palestinians (worldwide) has increased by six and half times since 1948, the Jewish population (worldwide) only returned to its pre-WWII level in 2016. So if even half of the Palestinians alive today returned to the region, the Jewish population would be completely outnumbered, and would have to risk the fate of other minorities who currently live in majority Muslim states. Moreover, remember that in the same interval of time, i.e. from 1948 to the present, the average expectable lifespan for a Palestinian man has increased from 48 to 74 years of age. Please. This is *genocide*? While the Occupation and the theft of Palestinian lands is indeed reprehensible, and a black mark on Israel's human rights record, an unbiased appraisal of these numbers demonstrates the absurdity of efforts to equate the Israeli Occupation of Palestinian lands with the Nazis' genocidal intentions toward the Jewish people. The latter, which culminated in the Shoah (or Holocaust), was an expression of depravity on a whole other scale of magnitude. Nevertheless, at BDS gatherings, Israelis are incessantly compared to Nazis, and this rhetorical stance harms and hinders, rather than advances, the cause of peace.

So, is Zionism purely or primarily a "colonial-settler enterprise"? Or are Jews indigenous to the region as well? Historians confirm that after the Romans crushed the last Jewish rebellion, Jews managed to maintain a continuous presence in Palestine. Despite their subsequent dispersal in the first and second centuries CE, small communities of this largely disinherited people stayed on in Palestine as a religious minority under their Roman, Byzantine, Sasanian, Ummayad, Abbasid and Ottoman masters, and were granted *dhimmi* status by their Muslim rulers.

Another reason it is wrong to depict Zionism as an instance of White settler-colonialism is that many of the 850,000 Jews who fled Arab lands, and the 120,000 Jews who fled or were airlifted from (Christian) Ethiopia, were black or brown skinned people who had no place else to go. Refugees from Muslim countries more than doubled Israel's initial population of 650,000 by 1960, the year Neumann passed away, and Jews of color now comprise roughly 20% of Israel's population. Equating Zionism with White Supremacy, as many BDS supporters do, is thus a completely misguided premise. It overlooks the fact that black and brown skinned people have oppressed other black and brown skinned people because they were Jewish, i.e. were anti-Semitic; that anti-Semitism was not a uniquely European phenomenon.

Finally, it is important to remember that the vast majority of (White) Ashkenazi Jews who settled in Palestine were not primarily motived by greed, but by sheer desperation. Indeed, most of them were refugees fleeing for their very lives, much like the impoverished families from Central and South America who now throng to our southern border in a futile search for safety, asylum and a chance to rebuild their lives in freedom. Moreover, when they did gain admittance, often against formidable odds, and at considerable risk to their own safety, these refugees and illegal immigrants did not seize Palestinian lands by violence or force, but purchased them legally from local sheiks and effendis with funds provided by Jewish charities and philanthropists (Morris, 2001).

Furthermore, on reflection, there are some deeply disquieting parallels between the Mufti's attitudes toward Jewish refugees and illegal immigrants and those of Donald Trump today. Activists on the Left who are deeply (and rightly) appalled by the xenophobia and racism exhibited by the Trump administration are often oblivious to the fact that most Jewish "settlers" who landed in British mandated Palestine before and after WWII were fleeing racism and White Supremacy in its most lethal forms, and were often met by extreme xenophobia and mistrust from the Palestinian population and their leaders, many of whom sided (or sympathized) with Hitler.

So, much as I deplore the violence of the Occupation, I am appalled at the rhetoric that BDS activists use with reference to Israel and Zionism, especially in speeches and public gatherings where participants compare or equate all Zionists with Nazis or White Supremacists. The fact that this is a commonplace occurrence at BDS rallies and events belies the BDS organization's claim that they do not "target identity". On reflection, this claim is as deeply disingenuous as the claim that Palestinians cannot be anti-Semitic, i.e. hate Jews. Granted, the *leadership* of BDS sedulously avoid language that is overtly anti-Jewish. But their membership's hostility to Zionism is palpable at their rallies, where Jews who support Zionism in any form, i.e. the vast majority alive today, are vilified and dismissed by BDS opinion leaders in public gatherings. The BDS movement claims, in effect – though seldom in so many words, of course – that by virtue of their support for the existence of Israel, the majority of Jews are racist and/or colonialist, if not by intention then by default; that the only "good Jew" is an anti-Zionist or non-Zionist Jew. While the Palestinians have plenty of legitimate grievances, to be sure, this carefully crafted BDS platform is merely another expression of low-intensity/high-brow anti-Semitism, cleverly disguised in the language of human rights. Their attitudes, in turn, have had a profound on the Black Lives Matter movement, where sadly, anti-Semitic attitudes still flourish, fomenting hatred and mistrust.

Was it ever thus? No, not at all. In the 1960s, Martin Luther King Jr. was a strong supporter of Israel, and said that anti-Zionism is often a disguise for anti-Semitism. Does that make him a White Supremacist, or an accomplice to genocide? I suppose that depends on your historical perspective. From the standpoint of many anti-racist activists nowadays, Rev. King's support for Israel were probably symptomatic of a dreadful blind-spot or of hopeless naivete on his part. But Rev. King was not the only Black leader to support Israel in those days. So did Rosa Parks. In fact, on November 25, 1975, some seven years after King's murder, she and other Black leaders comprising the *Black Americans to Support Israel Committee* (BASIC) placed an ad in the *New York Times* which described Israel as a beacon of democracy in a region dominated by monarchies, theocracies and authoritarian regimes. This gesture was quite obviously a response to a UN Resolution that was passed on November 10, 1975 – (Resolution 3379) – which declared that "Zionism is racism". Their ad also supported the pursuit of peace through mutual recognition and the right of Palestinian self-determination, i.e. a two state solution. Significantly, people who signed this document included many respected community leaders, including Julian Bond, Rev. Ralph Abernathy, Bayard Rustin, Tom Bradley, Mrs. Louis Armstrong, Lionel Hampton, Hank Aron, Alfred Bright (the Director of African American Studies at Youngstown State) and Congresswoman Yvonne Braithwaite Burke, among others.

Needless to say, the Black Panthers and the Nation of Islam did not agree. In the mid-1970s, Stockley Carmichael and Louis Farakhan were ferocious critics of Israel, and also said blatantly anti-Semitic things in their public speeches. And so, indeed, did Rev. Jesse Jackson and Rev. Al Sharpton. Nevertheless, the fact remains that when the Black Americans for Support of Israel Committee signed their document, Israel actually *was* the closest thing to a genuine democracy in the region.

Sadly, the overall character of Israel has changed dramatically over the years. When Neumann died in 1960, the kibbutz movement was still growing, and a major influence in Israeli politics. Yes, Israel was a flawed society, struggling to integrate a vast influx of refugees from Arab countries and to bring Adolf Eichmann to justice. But in the early days of its existence, the corruption, religious fundamentalism and ethno-nationalism which are so pervasive and worrisome in Israel today were barely factors in Israeli politics. They only existed in the margins or on the periphery of Israeli society.

But in 1989, the year Kirsch died, and the year the *Lingering Shadows* conference convened at the New School, the kibbutz movement no longer had nearly the same impact on the Israeli government and elect-orate. Ironically, one reason the Kibbutz movement lost so much of its influence was the Law of Return, instituted when the state of Israel was founded on May 14, 1948. This law stated that Jews living anywhere in the world could immigrate (or make "aliyah") and come home to the land of their ancestors. As a result, over the years, Israel was inundated with hundreds of thousands of immigrants fleeing persecution from the Muslim world, from Ethiopia and the soon-to-be former Soviet Union. Though many of these immigrants transited through various kib-butzim, at one point or another, few took up permanent residence there, or shared the kibbutzniks political outlook and aspirations. Indeed, in time these immigrant communities and the political parties that they created tilted the balance of power away from Labour and toward the (secular) Right wing and religious parties, who have formed most of the governing coalitions in the Knesset (Israeli Parliament) since 1977.

So, sadly, since 1989, religious fundamentalism, corruption and an increasingly vicious ethno-nationalism have become much more preva-lent in Israeli politics. As a result, the government of Bibi Netanyahu is now annexing even more Palestinian territory, effectively nullifying the

Palestinian people's aspirations to statehood. In so doing, in a manner of speaking, they are replicating the trauma inflicted on the Jewish psyche by the Roman authorities in the first and second centuries. And when you pause to think about it, ironies abound here. It is precisely because of their brutal repression and dispersal by their Roman overlords two millennia ago that many activists repudiate the Jews' indigeneity, and with it, their right of return to their ancestral homeland or any portion thereof.

Besides, if Israel does *not* grant Palestinians full citizenship, as Barghouti and the BDS movement demand that it does, Israel will become what some call an apartheid state; a very serviceable analogy, especially if you construe Zionism, even the most progressive and peace-loving varieties, as instances of "White Supremacy". But for many inhabitants of this region, a more apt analogy is not South African style apartheid, but dhimmitude, i.e. a caste system based on faith, not "race". If Israel continues to deny Palestinians their basic human rights, they would be flipping the old status-quo ante on its head, and imposing second (or third class) citizenship on their former masters; a fact not lost on either party to this conflict, to be sure. But there is crucial difference here, because Palestinians living under Israeli sovereignty are not a small and powerless minority, as Jews in Muslim lands were. On the contrary, they are a large and powerful minority who – given current rates of population growth – will swiftly outnumber the Jews living in that region.

Leaving the ethical dimension aside, momentarily, the idea that this state of affairs would be tenable or sustainable in the long run, from either a political or a military standpoint, is simply delusional. Imposing a new version of dhimmitude on the Palestinian populace would invite punishing (though well deserved) trade sanctions, another massive *intifada* (or series of intifadas), and/or another regional war with Arab armies that would likely lead to Israel's destruction. Failure to recognize this represents a monumental lapse in judgment, a collective flight from reality, and only shows how angry, embittered and traumatized Jews were in the wake of the Holocaust and centuries of oppression by Romans, Christians and Muslims alike.

Obviously, this can't end well. The only workable solution to the Middle East problem (in the long run) is one that will anger and disappoint large numbers of extremists on *both* sides of the conflict. To make peace possible, Israelis must relinquish large tracts of land equivalent in size and value to those they seized in 1967, and permit a free and open corridor for travel between the West Bank and Gaza. The Palestinians, in turn, have to relinquish the Right of Return. Almost no one will be happy with this compromise, but it is the only one with any prospect of lasting success. Will this ever happen? God only knows. But if it does, perhaps one day the grandchildren of Israelis and Palestinians who are currently locked in mutual hatred and mistrust will greet one another in genuine fellowship. If it does not, the conflicts in this region will never, ever cease.

Notes

1 Though he is seldom cited in this literature nowadays, Jung was actually quite prescient on the subject of intergenerational transmission, having discovered that "complexes" are often transmitted unconsciously from parents to their children in his association experiments.
2 For an illuminating discussion of the Biblical concept of idolatry, see Erich Fromm's book *You Shall Be As Gods: A Radical Interpretation of the Old Testament and Its Tradition* (Fromm, 1966).
3 Obviously, this process was well advanced in Jesus' lifetime. As his ministry started in Galilee, it was primarily to these people whom he preached.
4 There were two clans competing for dominance in pre-WWII Palestine – the Husseini clan in Jerusalem and the south, and the Nashashibi clan, which had a smaller presence in Jerusalem, but dominated the northern part of the country. (A third clan, the Barghouti family, is from Ramallah and vicinity.)

References

Avineri, S. 1981. *The Making of Modern Zionism*. New York. Basic Books.
Elon, A. 2002. *The Pity of It All: A History of the Jews in Germany 1743–1933*. New York: Picador.
Flapan, S. 1987. *The birth of Israel: Myths and Realities*. New York: Pantheon.
Fromm, E. 1966. *You Shall Be As Gods: A Radical Interpretation of the Old Testament and Its Tradition*. Greewich, CT: Fawcett Premier Books.
Johnson, I. 2010. *A Mosque in Munich: Nazis, the CIA and the Rise of the Muslim Brotherhood in the West*. New York: Houghton Mifflin Harcourt.
Julius, L. 2020. *Uprooted: How 3,000 Years of Jewish Civilization in the Arab World Vanished Overnight*. London: Vallentine Mitchell.
Lacquer, W. 2006. *The Changing Face of Anti-Semitism*. New York: Oxford University Press.
Lammers, A.C. ed., 2011. *The Jung-Kirsch Letters: The Correspondence of C.G. Jung and James Kirsch*. London: Routledge.
Liebscher, M. ed., 2015. *Analytical Psychology in Exile: The Correspondence of C.G. Jung and Erich Neumann*. Princeton, NJ: Princeton University Press.
Morris, B. 2001. *Righteous Victims: A History of the Zionist Arab Conflict*. New York: Random House.
Schwartz, A. and Wilf, E. 2020. *The War of Return: How Western Indulgence of the Palestinian Dream Has Obstructed the Path to Peace*. New York: All Points Books.

7   Anti-Semitism and the cultural unconscious

So, in light of the preceding, what can analytical psychology contribute to our understanding of the regional conflicts in Israel/Palestine? Nothing, I fear, if Jungians address these issues without a sound knowledge of the region, its peoples and their histories. Absent a deep and nuanced knowledge of the historical background, even seasoned clinicians will likely embrace or endorse the Israeli narrative or the Palestinian narrative uncritically, and empathize exclusively with one party in what is actually a very complex and morally ambiguous situation. This preempts the possibility of genuine dialogue, fostering unreasonable demands and collective flights from reality (on both sides). We've had more than enough of that already. Realism must prevail for peace to occur, and for all those whose lives are enmeshed in this hellish and seemingly intractable conflict to finally give peace a chance.

Nevertheless, there is one Jungian concept that provides a useful template for understanding certain aspects of the Israeli/Palestinian conflict, and may help point the way toward an eventual resolution. Specifically, one could interpret aspects of the Israeli/Palestinian conflict in terms of competing and (mutually reinforcing) "cultural complexes". The term "cultural complex" was invented by Joseph Henderson in December 1947, in correspondence with C.G. Jung, when he stated his intention of writing a book about "Protestant Man". As Thomas Singer and Catherine Kaplinsky point out, Henderson never finished this book, or developed the corresponding concept of the "cultural unconscious" in full. Moreover, because of what they graciously term Jung's "ill-timed foray" into discussions of national character in the 1930s, Jung's followers stopped exploring or explaining differences between groups of people on the basis of race, ethnicity and tribal/national identities after WWII. Nevertheless, say Singer and Kaplinsky, recent reflections on Jung's attitude toward Jews, i.e. the *Lingering Shadows* conference and its aftermath, have freed up more theorists to resume exploration of the "cultural unconscious" – this time, presumably, without the racist and anti-Semitic biases that rendered Jung's initial efforts in this direction so problematic (Singer and Kaplinsky, 2010).

The cultural unconscious is defined as an area of unconscious mentation wedged between the personal and collective unconscious, though it communicates with them both. Cultural complexes are defined as "emotionally charged aggregates of ideas and images that tend to cluster around an archetypal core" shared by individual members of particular collectives. Still, Singer and Kaplinsky say, Jungians must "resist the typical temptation to reduce every group conflict to an archetypal motif", giving more consideration to the uniqueness of different cultures. According to Singer and Kaplinsky:

> Cultural complexes are based on frequently repeated historical experiences that have taken root in the collective psyche ... and express archetypal values for the group. As such, cultural complexes can be thought of as fundamental building blocks of an inner sociology.
>
> (p. 6)

They go on to point out that cultural complexes:

> enshrine and encrust themselves in the consciousness and unconscious of groups of people ... Simultaneously, they intertwine themselves with the cultural complexes of other groups ... Indeed, these intertwining and affect laden energies of conflicting unconscious cultural complexes can form the preconditions for human events to unfold with a fury that can be likened to (natural disasters).
>
> (p. 19)

While Singer and Kaplinsky do not address themselves to the Israeli/Palestinian conflict specifically, they note that the Muslim world has entered a period of protracted conflict with the West; a conflict which, I would argue, profoundly complicates the Israeli/Palestinian one. They note, for example that

> (The year) 1492 ... marks the beginning of the retreat of Islam from the West and a long steady decline for the past 500 years of Islam's ability to take creative initiative in the intellectual, economic and social realms. This decline in Islamic power and influence has led to a cultural complex in the Islamic world and especially in its groups

of radical fundamentalists that can be characterized by 1) adherence to purity, 2) adherence to absolutism, 3) adherence to tradition, 4) adherence to incorruptibility.

(p. 21)

Singer and Kaplinsky also note what they call

a profound wound at the center of its group spirit that has given rise to despair and suicidal self-destructiveness. Repeated humiliation is at the heart of the Arab world's experience of itself, and the fear and rage at humiliation constitutes a most dangerous core symptom of the Islamic cultural complex.

(p. 22)

We recently saw that fear, rage and humiliation unleashed on Iraqi Christians, who were blamed indiscriminately for the Second Iraq Invasion. Christians in Iraq numbered more than 1.4 million before 2003, but in 2019, numbered less than 250,000. The current flight of indigenous Christians from other Middle Eastern and North African countries follows a similar pattern.

So, Singer and Kaplinsky's description of Islamic fundamentalism is accurate and commendable, as far as it goes. But it neglects to point out that Islamism's rigid adherence to purity, absolutism, tradition (and so on) render it extremely intolerant and prone to violence. Even more curiously, they neglect to point out that the cultural unconscious of both the Christian and Islamic worlds are constellated in relation to Judaism *before* they become intertwined with each other, and that the lasting impact of that state of affairs still shapes most varieties of contemporary anti-Semitism.

That said, the following reflections on the cultural unconscious in Judaism, Christianity and Islam are drawn in very broad strokes, and do not apply equally to all members of these faiths. On the contrary, there is considerable variation between individuals, depending on their levels of acculturation and individuation. There are also significant differences among the different denominations of these faiths, and in one and the same denomination in different historical periods. There are also profound regional variations, where one and the same faith and set of sacred scriptures are lived and interpreted very differently for a wide variety of reasons. Obviously, we can't do all of them justice here.

With those caveats in mind, however, please note that, in Singer and Kaplinsky's rendering, the cultural unconscious consists (in part) of "frequently repeated historical experiences that have taken root in the collective psyche ...". That being so, it is significant that – among other things, of course – the Hebrew Bible chronicles patterns of displacement and migration that are repeated over many hundreds of years. We are told, for example, that almost 6,000 years ago, Adam and Eve were banished from Eden to roam the face of the earth. Abraham, the first patriarch, leaves Ur and journeys south and west to Canaan, his patrimony. Joseph, son of Jacob, the third patriarch, is taken to Egypt, and is followed shortly thereafter by his brothers, whose families and clans move south to escape a deadly drought, only to leave later, escaping slavery to an anonymous Pharoah. After wandering in the wilderness for 40 years under Moses' leadership, the Israelites return to their Promised Land, only to be exiled again by the Babylonians, who destroy their Temple in 586 BCE. They return (again) to rebuild under Persian sovereignty in 516 BCE. After another 585 years, the Romans destroy their second Temple in 70 CE, and in 135 CE, exile the Jews from Jerusalem, their Holy City.

Similar patterns pervade Jewish history in the post-Biblical era; persecution, exile, migration, persecution, exile, migration – from England, Iberia, North Africa, Germany and many other lands. Only restoration to "the Promised Land" from the Biblical narrative was omitted, or more precisely, held in suspension for almost two millennia. In the midst of these bloody and tumultuous comings and goings, Abraham's progeny remained engaged in a binding covenant with their Creator, Judge and Redeemer – known variously as Elohim, Adonai, Ha'Shem, etc. – as they awaited the arrival of a Messiah who will inaugurate a universal kingdom of peace, prosperity and brotherhood, where war and poverty will cease. And as they waited for his arrival, the Jews deflected their mother-centered libido (which is detached from the soil) toward other devotional objects that were now personified as feminine; the Torah, coeternal wife of God; the Sabbath Queen, the Shechinah, etc., all of which are expressions of the mother archetype.

Though it differs from Judaism in several fundamental respects, the fact remains that Christianity owes its very existence to Judaism. Indeed, its collective narrative and sacred scriptures only cohere *in relationship to Judaism*. Yet beginning with St. Paul, Christian theologians claimed that the Mosaic covenant has been superseded, and that Christian believers, who comprise the Church, are now "God's beloved people". This "replacement theology" masks an underlying resentment born of dependence, because in the final analysis, Christianity cannot exist without Judaism – though the reverse is obviously not the case. Christian anti-Semites recoil against this realization by claiming that Jews lack a culture of their own, are parasitic on other cultures, or that are spiritually deficient, kill their own prophets, even as they borrowed freely from pagan religions when it suited their purposes. The Christian anti-Semite's need to demonize or dismiss members of the Jewish faith is thus rooted in fears and feelings that are seldom conscious, but are part of what may be called Christendom's cultural unconscious, which the modern, Western world has inherited willy-nilly. We know this because of the recent resurgence of anti-Semitism in the West, despite the cultural crises and growing pains that gave it a decisive cultural, scientific, economic and military advantage over the Islamic world. These included the Renaissance, the Reformation, the Scientific and the Industrial Revolutions, and the crucial separation between Church and State, which is absent in most Muslim societies, where politics and religion form a seamless continuum, and traditions of democratic governance have yet to take root.

The cultural unconscious of the Islamic world is also constellated around its relationship to Judaism, although here another kind of replacement theology and triumphalism are at work. Unlike Christianity, Islam does not deny that Jews may be justified in God's eyes on the Day of Judgment, nor do they view Jesus as the Messiah. But their scripture, the Koran, depicts many, if not most Jews as treacherous and hypocritical, and declares Mohammad's followers to be God's chosen people. That being so, Muslims felt – and for the most part, still feel – entitled to consign members of the Jewish faith to dhimmitude in lands where they constitute the majority. So, in addition to all the old reasons for distrusting and disparaging Jews, the Zionist project of a sovereign majority-Jewish state threatens to turn their religious cosmology upside down by demoting *them* to dhimmi status, even if it is only in a tiny corner of the world; a development they deem to be unnatural and contrary to God's law.

Thinking by analogy to the Christian West, which we explored in Chapter 1, we might say that Islamic fundamentalists are low-brow/high-intensity anti-Semites, while some Boycott, Divest and Sanction movement spokespeople, who profess to deplore violence, and sedulously avoid open expressions of anti-Semitism, represent the high-brow/low-intensity variety. What makes them anti-Semitic is not their condemnation of the current Israeli government, which is riddled with racism and corruption, and deserving of condemnation on many counts. It is their eagerness to grant the right of national self-determination to the Palestinian people while denying it to the Jews, condemning them to dhimmitude (albeit by new names, perhaps), coupled with their sweeping claim that Zionism in *all* its forms is intrinsically racist and imperialist. But for better or worse, by dint of their tragic history, the majority of Jews living today are still Zionists, so saying that "Zionism is racism" (or equivalent to White Supremacy) is tantamount to saying that the majority of Jews today are White racists. This extravagant claim *might* be remotely credible or at least tolerable in civil discourse if those making it also conceded how prevalent, intense and deeply rooted anti-Semitism in the Muslim world is. But that seldom –if ever – is the case. Instead, if anyone dares to point this out, they are usually greeted with vehement denials and hostile charges of Islamophobia.

Moreover, and more to the point perhaps, this way of framing the Zionist project replicates an ancient pattern in the Koran, where the majority of Jews are doomed to perdition on account of their treachery and hypocrisy. Now, as then, "good Jews" are accounted to be a small minority. But who decides who is a "good Jew"? Jews themselves? According to their own criteria? Perish the thought! No, instead, a vast coalition of Muslims – and their allies and surrogates on the Left, including some of Jewish heritage – are somehow authorized to determine who is or is not a "good Jew", according to their own (explicitly anti-Zionist) criteria. The isomorphism between this rhetorical strategy and the attitude in the Koran is glaringly obvious, hiding in plain sight.

How did the Left become so deeply imbricated in and infused with Muslim anti-Semitism? One factor to consider is that Left leaning movements and political parties have traditionally played a more active and prominent role in British and European politics than they have in the United States, where socialism is still a dirty word, evoking fear and hostility in many quarters. However, faced with their steadily declining power and popularity, and the recent resurgence of Right-wing populism, Left leaning Europeans often make common cause with marginalized and oppressed groups; the very same groups that the extreme Right reviles.

Meanwhile, since the end of WWII, Islamism has established a strong foothold in many impoverished and marginalized Muslim communities in Europe, where several generations have grown up in Muslim "ghettos" without ever feeling welcomed or integrated into the cultural mainstream. In many ways, the lived experience of most Muslims growing up in Europe is similar to those of stateless Palestinians living in refugee camps. So the extreme Left champions them because Muslims are often the target of vicious Right-wing attacks, and because the Islamists in their midst vigorously denounce the powers that be. The result?

The Vienna-based *European Union Agency for Fundamental Rights* or *Fundamental Rights Agency* (FRA) conducted a survey of 12 European countries and the United Kingdom in 2018. The survey disclosed that victims of anti-Semitic harassment or persecution identified 30% of the perpetrators as Muslim extremists, another 21% as Left-wing extremists, and only 13% as Right-wing extremists – a truly startling finding. It also found that the three most common justifications for anti-Semitic hatred were that "Jews behave like Nazis towards the Palestinians", "Jews have too much power" and "Jews exploit Holocaust victimhood for their own purposes".

That being said, these figures are averaged out among 13 countries, and taken in the aggregate, tend to obscure the considerable variation that obtains from one country to the next. So, for example, 53% of Polish Jews and 46% of Hungarian Jews identified "someone with a right-wing political view" as the typical aggressor, compared to 20% of Jews in Germany, 11% in the United Kingdom and 7% in France. Moreover, 41% of German Jews and 33% of French Jews said "someone with a Muslim extremist view" was the perpetrator, compared to just 2% of Polish and Hungarian Jews, which demonstrates a clear correlation between the size of the country's Muslim population and the severity of the violence committed against Jews by non-Right-wing actors.

Further studies are needed before we can establish how accurate these findings are. But the fact that Left-wing and Muslim aggression accounts for roughly half of the *experienced* anti-Semitism in Europe and the United Kingdom today stands in stark contrast to the situation in the United States, where the Muslim population is smaller, and the majority of hate crimes against Jews are still committed by White Supremacists of one stripe or another. It also stands in stark contrast to the situation in Europe in the 1930s. Anti-Semitic violence was as prevalent then as it is now, but its sources and sponsors were quite different. In the 1930s, hate crimes against European Jews were committed overwhelmingly by far Right agents and activists. Hate crimes by Muslims and far Left activists against Jewish communities in Europe during the 1930s were probably a mere fraction of the total.

And what about the United States? Americans take some solace knowing that they are less anti-Semitic, on average, than their European counterparts. But for how long? After all, there are plenty of disturbing signs that the United States is following in Europe's footsteps, only at a slightly slower pace. Because of the length and brutality of the Israeli occupation, the Palestinian narrative – predictably enough – is winning more hearts and minds in the United States than it did in the 20th century. This is doubtless because (1) Israelis have the upper hand both economically and militarily (for now), and (2) many anti-racist activists nowadays equate Zionism with White Supremacy, or treat it merely as a straightforward instance of White settler colonialism, designed to rob the indigenous population of their lands, their livelihoods, their dignity and their future. These characterizations are false or exaggerated, in the final analysis, but they are gaining more public sympathy and support. This is not only true among Gentiles, but among many young Jews in the diaspora, who are rejecting their parents' Zionism in unprecedented numbers.

That being so, it bears remembering that much as they are opposed in their attitudes toward Islamism and Israel/Palestine, Right- and Left-wing anti-Semites *on both sides of the Atlantic* actively share memes and conspiracy theories that scapegoat Jews, focusing collective hatred onto a tiny minority of the general population. This fact has startled many recent commentators, for whom this is a novel discovery, but it is actually nothing new. On the contrary, it predates the founding of Israel by more than a century. In the 19th century, Eugen Dühring, Pierre-Joseph Proudhon and Mikhail Bakunin characterized Jews as an international cabal of exploiters and war profiteers, just as their Right-wing counterparts did – and indeed, still do. Karl Marx's essay "On the Jewish Question" (1845) is riddled with anti-Semitic stereotypes, and Richard Wagner, a notorious anti-Semite, started out as a Left-winger, only to morph into a proto-Nazi as he rose to fame. And of course Joseph Stalin was a vicious anti-Semite, both before and after the founding of Israel.

Nevertheless, many Leftists – including some who are Jewish! – vehemently deny or minimize their own anti-Semitic biases, and imagine that anti-Semitism is a uniquely Right-wing phenomenon, and insist that support for Islamist organizations is a perfectly valid response to Israel's human rights abuses. But as Slavoj Žižek reminds us, it is

> all too easy and uncritical acceptance of anti-American and anti-Western Muslim groups as representing "progressive" forms of struggle, as automatic allies; groups like Hamas and Hezbollah suddenly appear as revolutionary agents, even though their ideology is explicitly anti-modern, rejecting the entire egalitarian legacy of the French Revolution.
>
> (Žižek, 2011, p. 137)

Žižek has a point. When all is said and done, the leaders of Hamas and Hezbollah are fundamentalists who pay lip service to the rhetoric of human rights when it serves their purposes, but ignore them completely when it does not. They are demonstrably and unabashedly misogynistic, anti-gay and anti-democratic. And they are *not* merely anti-Zionist, but fiercely anti-Semitic, because they engage in Holocaust minimization and denial, or else claim that the Jews brought the Holocaust on themselves; an unmistakable anti-Semitic trope. They also endorse *The Protocols of the Elders of Zion* as an authentic historical document, rather than the vicious slander that it is.

So, to summarize, Right-wing racists abhor multiculturalism and promote Islamophobia, stressing the incommensurability between Islamic values and what they call "Western civilization". They also celebrate and revel in their capacity to injure and humiliate their (real and imaginary) racial foes. By contrast with their Right-wing counterparts, the far Left – which prides itself on being anti-racist – espouses a strange brand of multiculturalism that completely excludes Jews (if they are Zionists) and devalues or ignores Jewish experience, but often *embraces* Islamist organizations in what it imagines is a progressive, anti-imperialist coalition. In this way, the Left can champion the putative underdog – adhering to the Left's traditional role – while sanctioning violence *indirectly*, as well as aggressively targeting, vilifying and dismissing anyone who disagrees openly and emphatically with their one-sided world view.

So, this is the predicament of contemporary Jewry. Even the most progressive Jews today are caught between increasingly belligerent extremists on the Right and the Left. The common ground between these passionate adversaries resides chiefly in their attraction to bizarre conspiracy theories, and their tendencies to blame Jews and/or Israel in absurd and far-fetched ways for many of the evils that are endemic in their own societies. For Jewish people, regardless of their political leanings, the storm clouds now gathering on the horizon look all too familiar. We've seen them many times before, long before the state of Israel was established. People unfamiliar with Jewish history may be inclined to attribute the current resurgence of anti-Semitism to the failure of peace talks in the Middle East, which they blame entirely on Israel. The truth, of course, is far more complex (Schwartz and Wilf, 2020). But if a just solution to the situation there did materialize, most of the pretexts that mask anti-Semitic attitudes on the Left would vanish. The most hopeful development in recent decades is the emergence of a new paradigm for peace supported by equal numbers of Israelis and Palestinians. Their plan is to create two coequal states in Israel and Palestine; states that share Jerusalem as their capital, and form a federation which permits complete freedom of movement and equal rights among their citizens. It goes by the name of "One Land for All", and shows more realism and good will than any other strategy or initiative currently in play.

Meanwhile, odd as it sounds, as the Jungian world's political center of gravity drifted away from Jung's curious conservatism, Israel's political center of gravity drifted in the opposite direction, toward the far Right. As a result, anti-Semitism of the Left-wing variety occurs in Jungian circles, too. Given the history of Analytic Psychology, contemporary Jungians should be mindful of the sins and errors of the past, and take the re-emergence of global anti-Semitism seriously, so that they do not stand idly by or reinforce potentially lethal cultural trends. And this duty obviously includes addressing anti-Semitism when it arises among their own members and affiliates; something most were formerly unwilling or unable to do.

References

Schwartz, A. and Wilf, E. 2020. *The War of Return: How Western Indulgence of the Palestinian Dream Has Obstructed the Path to Peace*. New York: All Points Books.

Singer, T. and Kaplinsky, C. 2010. "Cultural Complexes in Analysis." In *Jungian Psychoanalysis: Working in the Spirit of C.G.Jung*", ed. Murray Stein, pp. 22–27. Chicago: Open Court Publishing.

Žižek, S. 2011. *Living in the End Times*. London: Verso.

Index

Printed in the United States
by Baker & Taylor Publisher Services